A PHILOSOPHY OF HOPE

T0246774

A Philosophy of Hope

Lars Svendsen

Translated by Matt Bagguley

REAKTION BOOKS

Published by
REAKTION BOOKS LTD
Unit 32, Waterside
44–48 Wharf Road
London N1 7UX, UK
www.reaktionbooks.co.uk

First published by Kagge, 2023 as *Håpets filosofi*
English-language translation © Reaktion Books 2024

Matt Bagguley asserts his moral right to be identified
as the translator of the work

Copyright © Lars H. Fr. Svendsen 2023
Published in agreement with Oslo Literary Agency

This translation has been published
with the financial support of NORLA

Printed and bound in Great Britain
by Bell & Bain, Glasgow

A catalogue record for this book is available
from the British Library

ISBN 978 1 78914 943 2

Contents

Introduction

Human life is saturated with hope. It is hard to imagine a human that doesn't hope and yet still functions. You can always be alive without hope, albeit without really living. Humans are also, as far as we know, the only animals that hope, the reason being that hope is intrinsically linked to so many other characteristics we tend to believe are unique to humans. For example, a requirement for hope is language. Hope is also a far more complex phenomenon than we – and most philosophers throughout history – typically assume. It is precisely because hope is so fundamental, and a part of almost every task we undertake, that we easily lose sight of it by taking it somewhat for granted. But on closer inspection we find that this phenomenon is quite tricky to understand. Hope isn't something that suddenly appears from thin air in your emotional life. It has to be learned and developed. It is often referred to as a feeling, and although hope undoubtedly has an emotional side it is probably just as connected to reason as is to feelings. As such, hoping is neither rational nor irrational, and it can be done both well and badly. Hope is in no way the same as optimism; one can be both pessimistic and hopeful at the same time. You can be a functioning pessimist, but without hope you simply will not live a fully human life.

My books have always been motivated by hope. To write is to map and delineate something not properly understood in the hope of finally attaining the clarity one seeks. Sometimes it works out as you'd hoped, sometimes it doesn't. This time, it is hope itself that I've set out to understand. It's also time that I write this book, the seed of which may have been planted when I was completing my earlier book about fear. The first draft ended with: 'Perhaps what we need – and what I should have written – is a philosophy of hope rather than a philosophy of fear.' That sentence, however, was cut before the book was published, and the idea remained unprocessed for fifteen years.

The direct reason why the subject came back to me was Russia's invasion of Ukraine on 24 February 2022. What prompted me above all else to write this little book about hope was the way the Ukrainian people responded. There were of course many different emotions within the population, such as rage, despair, grief and so on, but the most prominent emotion seemed to be the hope that they would be able to withstand this attack from the Russian superpower and preserve their freedom.

At the same time, I wondered if this hope might just be a form of madness given the Russian military might that the Ukrainians were facing. It was perhaps reminiscent of the Athenian campaign against Melos, as described by the Greek historian Thucydides, where the Melians place their trust in hope rather than surrender to the superior Athenian army. The Melians believe that they have justice on their side (and they are probably right), but they also conclude that the gods might come to the defence of just world order, and it is this hope of divine intervention that motivates them to fight the superior force. The Athenians are unimpressed by the Melians' assessment and say that while hope is comforting in times of need it is simply ruinous to indulge in hope when it prevents one from acknowledging the situation one is actually in.[1] Instead of helping the Melians, hope will destroy them, the Athenians claim. And they were right. After a months-long siege of Melos, events went as follows: 'Of the Melian population the Athenians executed all the grown men who came into their hands and enslaved the children and women.'[2] The moral here is that trusting in hope is little more than a form of irrationality that leads to one's downfall. Hope isn't necessarily a good thing, and the hope of victory can lead to a far more brutal defeat.

The shortcoming that led to the Melians' downfall was not that they felt incorrectly, but that they had a faulty understanding of reality. The problem wasn't that they had hoped, but that they had hoped poorly. Their hope had blinded them to the fact that they were doomed to lose. Hope locked them into one vision of the future, namely that with divine assistance they would prevail. Had they hoped with more wisdom, it's possible that they may have acted – and lost – better, in a way that was less self-destructive.

There can be little doubt that the Ukrainian hope created a level of bravery and resistance that surpassed what anyone, not least the Russians, thought was possible, and it stopped the advance on Kyiv to replace the Ukrainian government with Russian puppets. In the short term, the Ukrainian hope has undoubtedly been a good thing, not least because this hope spurred other countries into providing the Ukrainians with weapons they would have been quite helpless without. In the longer term, all I can say is that I hope this will continue to be the case, although to genuinely hope that the Ukrainian people will succeed in their struggle demands something from us. Ukrainian hope has mobilized the people to fight – hope fosters actions that increase the likelihood that things will turn out as hoped for. But if we really are hoping for the same thing as the Ukrainian people, we too must act in a way that demonstrates that our hope is more than empty words: we must assist them in their struggle even if it costs us something, and only at a fraction of what it costs the Ukrainians. Hope obliges.

I see hope in one form or another to be unavoidable in normal human life. But whether hope is a blessing or a curse for us isn't obvious. In the myth of Pandora, as told by the Greek poet Hesiod, Pandora – which, ironically, means 'all-gifted' – is given a closed jar as a gift. Pandora herself is then given to Prometheus' slightly naive brother Epimetheus as a disguised punishment for Prometheus stealing fire from the gods. The two brothers' names are significant: Prometheus signifies 'foresight', while Epimetheus signifies 'hindsight'. Prometheus knows that no gift from Zeus is ever good, but his brother isn't so bright and happily accepts both Pandora and her jar. Pandora isn't the sharpest knife in the drawer either, and, despite being warned not to, opens the jar, unleashing all the world's evils – disease, suffering, grief and vice – on the people, who have until then lived without all these things but whose lives would now be troubled. When Pandora sees what she has unleashed on the world, she puts the lid back on as fast as possible, but by then there is only one thing left in the jar, and that is hope.

> For previously the tribes of men used to live upon the earth entirely apart from evils, and without grievous toil and distressful diseases, which give death to men. But the woman removed the great lid from the storage jar with her hands and scattered all its contents abroad – she wrought baneful evils for human beings. Only Hope remained there in its unbreakable home under the mouth of the storage jar, and did not fly out.[3]

How are we to understand this story? Was hope to be regarded as another evil from which humankind had been spared? Or was it in the jar to sweeten the bitter pill? In antiquity this was already a hotly debated topic, but the myth says nothing about it. The myth is in fact told so sparingly that it offers few clues as to what the correct interpretation should be, if such a thing actually exists.

The most widespread view is that the jar contained many evils and one good thing. Hope is good because it gives people a kind of grip on the future, and thus a degree of control over life. The gods do not need hope, since they know everything, and the animals cannot hope, since they are oblivious to their own impermanence. Man, however, who stands between the gods and the animals, has a need for hope. Since hope remains in the jar, the myth can be interpreted as being that man is subjected to living without hope.

It is fitting that the myth is so open to interpretation because it is also debatable as to whether hope is good or bad for us. Hesiod himself seems to think that hope is an evil that makes men lazy and inclined to behave poorly.[4] The German philosopher Friedrich Nietzsche points out that the ancient Greeks' perception of hope differs from ours, and he is right about that, but when he summarizes their view that hope is 'blind and malicious', he is too one-sided.[5] Nietzsche himself goes even further than Hesiod, claiming that hope is in fact the greatest of all evils:

> For what Zeus wanted was that man, though never so tormented by the other evils, should nonetheless not throw life away but continue to let himself be tormented. To that end he gives men hope: it is in truth the worst of all evils, because it protracts the torment of men.[6]

Perhaps the hope in the jar is an evil sailing under a false flag, presenting itself as good to the people since people want to hope for a better future, but evil in that hope always leads to disappointment. Is hope simply opium for the masses?

The word 'hope' seems to have quite different meanings and value for different people. For some, to hope is to become passive, to stop believing that you can accomplish something yourself and instead indulge in a belief that external forces will ensure things go as you wish; for others, hope is active and linked to creating possibilities, seen in an as yet undetermined future, a reality. Hope can be both of these things. 'Hope' can also be used in many different ways and in a variety of contexts, from the extremely trivial to the deeply existential. As I write this book, I hope that the end result will be good. I also hope that my wife and daughter get home safely from London despite the chaotic air travel situation caused by striking employees and so on. I hope that I never get kidney stones or gallstones again. I hope that Ukraine will be able to stand up to Russia's aggression. I hope it won't rain tomorrow, even though there are storms forecast, because I want to play tennis. I hope for happiness, both my own and for other people. I hope alone, but also with other people. I hope that other people will keep a promise, for example. We must hope for others when we are engaged in collective activities, that they too hope and act like us, so that our common goals can be achieved. I hope that we are not heading into a full-blown recession, with the immediate consequences it will have on too many people's quality of life and, in the next instance, on the political stability of the world. I hope that the trend we have seen of the gradual weakening of liberal democracy in country after country will be reversed. I hope that we will be able to slow down, and preferably stop, global warming and that we will be able to handle the approaching changes in climate. Sometimes I hope strongly, other times faintly; it can occupy most of my attention or be something I give very little thought to. I also have a more general hope, which could be confused with optimism, that the future will give reason for hope, that it holds significant opportunities even if the world situation perhaps seems gloomy right now. Is there any unity in these various forms of hope? Is there a lowest common denominator, or two? Will such a common denominator then give us a better understanding of what hope is?

Philosophical writings on hope are limited because philosophers have been largely quite sceptical about the phenomenon, which is probably due to the fact that they tend to be fond of certainty and absolutes, while hope is uncertain and limited. Hope is mentioned by many philosophers, although rarely given a more comprehensive analysis. But while hope isn't one of the most analysed concepts in philosophical literature, I still have to be selective. For example, I have chosen not to place significant emphasis on what is probably the most comprehensive work written about hope, *The Principle of Hope* (1954–9) by the German Marxist Ernst Bloch, for the simple reason that I do not think it can significantly contribute to enlightening us on how hope should be understood, despite the fact that Bloch discusses hope in detail over 1,500 pages. I am inclined to say that the insight one can gain from the work is inversely proportional to its length, in that it consists of a seemingly endless series of analyses of various cultural phenomena with flimsy Marxist metaphysics as a recurring theme. Having said that, there are some things Bloch writes that I can wholeheartedly agree with:

> It is a question of learning hope. Its work does not renounce, it is in love with success rather than failure. Hope, superior to fear, is neither passive like the latter, nor locked into nothingness. The emotion of hope goes out of itself, makes people broad instead of confining them.[7]

In the past the phenomenon of hope was most often dealt with by more continental philosophical thinkers with an existentialist or religious perspective. In recent decades the field has become more dominant among more analytical philosophers. The latter have brought significantly more precision to the philosophical debate about hope, which is no doubt highly valuable since philosophers work primarily with concepts, but it means that the debate has often been rather myopic and has revolved around meticulous discussions on how hope should be defined. There is little agreement on a definition in the literature. What you find instead is a somewhat chaotic variety of different attempts to define it. My goal, however, is not to arrive at a new definition of hope either, but to offer a broad description of hope's place in human life.[8]

The first three chapters of this book are as complicating as they are clarifying. In philosophy, you often find that what seems complicated at first glance is quite simple upon closer inspection. Conversely, apparently simple things can often turn out to be quite demanding when you delve beneath the surface. Hope is an example of that. What hope is may seem obvious, but when we think about it, this obviousness evaporates. The initial chapters are therefore devoted to showing how complex this phenomenon is, to give us a better picture of hope in general. There are some uncontroversial points – for example, that hope must revolve around the possible, that which is neither certain nor impossible. But after that, the challenges begin. Should hope be described as an emotion, or is it something else? Can other animals hope too? If not, why not? Many people claim that hope is an expression of irrationality, but I would argue that hope can be highly rational, and furthermore that a person who hopes actually increases the probability of a desired outcome. In Chapter Four I discuss the relationship between hope, determinism and freedom, my 'opponent' being Baruch Spinoza, who claimed that hope makes you unfree and that the path to freedom is to realize that all things happen with strict natural necessity. I argue, however, that hope takes place in what's possible: in freedom, in our ability to create one future instead of another. We then look at the politics of hope in Chapter Five, how a free society must be based on hope rather than fear – and here I am actually in agreement with Spinoza. I may have established already that hope as such is not irrational, but hope can be disastrous if misplaced. Chapter Six therefore deals with a distinction that goes all the way back to Aristotle, between hoping well and hoping badly. This theme can be said to be continued in Chapter Seven, on eternal and temporal hope, where I argue that eternal or religious hope displaces secular or temporal hope – the kingdom of heaven depletes the earth of meaning. Immanuel Kant claimed that the question of what we can hope for is one of the three main questions of philosophy, and in Chapter Eight we will look more closely at how he answered this question himself – the letters Kant received from a young woman asking for advice reveal not least that his answers were, at the end of the day, not particularly satisfying. Hope and optimism are often confused, but Chapter Nine also shows how you can undoubtedly be a hopeful pessimist – the decisive factor for hope is that the future is open. Whether you are pessimistic or optimistic, I maintain that you have a duty to be hopeful. Hope is a duty you have to yourself because it is a requirement for living a life that really is worth living. Hope can also be lost, and Chapter Ten attempts to describe in more detail what that entails. The analysis of the loss of hope also reveals that hope has two levels: one where we hope for this and that, and another, more fundamental level where we perceive the world to be somewhere hope is generally possible. In Chapter Eleven we come to the point that all the previous chapters have, in a sense, built up to, where I try to show that hope is a requirement for life to have meaning. Life puts us all to the test, but hope gives a person something attainable to focus on, something that transcends the pain experienced here and now. Hope has no way of magically reshaping the world to comply with your wishes, but it can move you – and therefore everyone – in the right direction.

This book provides a broad description of many aspects of hope. The biggest job, however, is left up to the reader: to assess what relevance this may have for his or her life. Philosophy, after all is said and done, is about self-examination, working on one's own thoughts and ways of looking at things, and for this work to have real value it must play a role in how one chooses to live. Such self-knowledge isn't something I can provide others with – every individual must acquire that for themselves. The most I can do is offer some perspectives that allow a reader to think something as yet unthought, or see something previously overlooked.

ONE

What Is Hope?

'Hope', as the word is used today, is linked to a good outcome. This is in contrast to the ancient Greek word *elpis*, which denoted visions of the future that could be negative, positive or value-neutral.[1] *Elpis* is therefore not entirely synonymous with what we call hope, but like hope it must be linked to an outcome that is neither certain nor impossible. It should be noted that the decisive factor here is the subjective uncertainty. For example, I have such a poor understanding of some causal relationships that I can believe X is possible, albeit unlikely, when in reality it is totally impossible. In that case, I can hope for X. If someone were to point out to me that X is not actually possible, and I accept that to be the case, I can no longer hope for X but I can still wish that it were possible. In the same way, I cannot hope that X will happen if I am totally convinced that it actually *will* happen. I would then be in a state of certainty rather than hopefulness.

You Can Only Hope for What Is Possible

Hope is contingent on there being a real possibility, but this real possibility must be understood as entirely subjective based on what an individual perceives to be really possible. In everyday speech, we use 'wish' and 'hope' interchangeably, which is normally no problem. If we want to draw a more precise distinction between them, we can say they are both aimed at something perceived to be positive, but not certain to be achievable. The difference is that I can only hope for something that I perceive to be possible; wishing does not have that limitation. For example, I might wish that I was able to levitate so that I could float around my office reading philosophy, but I can't hope to do so, simply because I know that gravity makes it impossible. In that sense, I can wish for almost everything that I hope for, but I cannot hope for everything that I wish for. How high should the likelihood of something be for it to be considered a hope? In principle there is no limit to how low the likelihood can be as long as it is above zero.

A person who really hopes will act, reflect and express themselves differently to a person who only wishes. A person who hopes is moving towards the goal. Hope will often be linked to one's own actions: if I do A, I hope that B happens. Hope can also apply to situations that are totally dependent on external factors you have no influence over. For example, I might buy a lottery ticket and hope to win a big prize that will end all my financial worries, but I have no way of influencing whether I win or not. We can call one active and the other passive hope. Perhaps hoping can be considered a midpoint between wishing and wanting. It is more than wishing because it has to be possible, but it is less than wanting because I am not sure if it can be carried out – it is not simply dependent on my capacity for agency.

The difference between hope and wishful thinking is that I don't have to deal with any realities as long as I'm in the wishful thinking domain. Wishful thinking is not limited by what's really possible – it's enough for something to be logically possible, that is, imaginable. Hope, on the other hand, must be limited to what really is possible. The wishful thinker can imagine something occurring as if by magic, while the person hoping also has to relate to how something can actually become real.

Hope must therefore be linked to something uncertain. As Paul correctly points out in his letter to the Romans: 'For in this hope we were saved. But hope that is seen is no hope at all. Who hopes for what they already have?' (8:24). Accounts of hope often assume that hope can only be directed at the future. For example, Aristotle writes that hope is, by definition, linked to the future, while everything in the past is linked to memory and everything in the present to sensing.[2] Although hope for the future is probably the most common, hope can also be linked to the past or present. What makes it hope isn't that it concerns something in the future, but that it is a desire for something that is only possible, not certain. I can hope that I didn't make too much a fool of myself when I got very drunk at a party the night before, for instance. Or if a friend who has been visiting drives home in a terrible storm, I can say: 'I hope she's made it back safely.' I can also hope that acquaintances I have in Kyiv don't get hit by the missiles raining down on the city as I write, or, to use a less dramatic example, that a friend makes a good impression in the job interview she is having now.

We can attempt to reformulate these examples so that they still concern something in the future, namely that my hope is that it will *turn out* that I did not make a fool of myself, that my guest made it home safely, that no one was hit by the missiles and that my friend made such a good impression that she got the job. In other words, we want to rewrite it in this form: 'I hope that it will turn out that X was the case,' where X is a past or present event, but where the hope itself is linked to a future confirmation. It doesn't solve much. I can, for instance, eagerly await the results of a study of Norwegian soldiers fighting for the Germans on the Eastern Front during the Second World War because my grandfather, with whom I always had a good relationship, was one of these front-line fighters. I fear that he was involved in serious abuses against civilians, but I hope that he wasn't. My hope is not only related to a future event where it will be documented that he was not involved in such atrocities. What's important is the past event: whether my grandfather actually did participate in any massacre. The rewriting of hope for the past to hope for the future is not convincing because the hope is particularly linked to the events themselves, to what actually happened, more than to the fact that in the future I will receive confirmation that X or Y is the case.

As for the example of being drunk at a party, my hope is not mainly that at some future point I'll be assured that I didn't make a fool of myself, although to a certain extent I can hope for that as well. My hope is that I haven't actually made a fool of myself. Hope linked to the past must necessarily be a passive hope since you cannot do anything to change it. The past is what it is. In order for the past to be an object of hope, what it was like has to be unclear. The past is determined, but as long as I have no reliable knowledge of what happened it is still in the domain of the subjectively possible and can therefore be an object of hope. If a friend of mine sends me a link to a video of the night before that clearly shows me embarrassing myself repeatedly, blind drunk, as the other guests watch the whole scene while shaking their heads, I will no longer be able to hope that I didn't make a fool of myself, since it is now an established fact that I did.

Hope that relates to the present or future can be active or passive. If I hope that I will make a good impression in the job interview I am currently sitting in, it will motivate me to make more effort to present my most advantageous side. Hope will then be active. If, however, I hope that my friend does well in the job interview she is currently having, it will be a passive hope since I can do nothing to influence how it goes. And while hope can be directed towards all three dimensions of time, it is most typically directed at the future, which is why I will be focusing on that specific hope in this book.

Hope must be linked to the notion of a state where something desirable happens, but where it is uncertain whether it can actually be achieved. You don't hope for something you are totally indifferent to. You can always feel uncertain about whether X or Y will occur, but if you do not care whether X or Y occurs, it cannot be said that you are hoping for X or Y.

Hope as a Feeling

Whether hope should be called a feeling naturally depends on what one understands feeling to be. In everyday speech hope is often referred to as a feeling, and while it no doubt has emotional aspects it also differs from most feelings since hope heavily involves rationality. If I hope that the kleptocrat Vladimir Putin will lose power, it doesn't just mean I want it to happen – it also means that I can imagine the real possibility that it will happen and preferably also have ideas about what it would take for that to happen. The point becomes perhaps even more apparent if we talk about 'losing hope'. Losing hope cannot be adequately described as just a certain feeling that has disappeared. Hope is also based on reasons, and when you lose hope you have also lost one or more reasons to hope.

The Austrian philosopher Ludwig Wittgenstein poses the question of whether it is the feeling that gives the expression 'hope' meaning:

> But when one says 'I *hope* he'll come' – doesn't the feeling give the word 'hope' its meaning? (And what about the sentence 'I do *not* hope for his coming any longer'?) The feeling does perhaps give the word 'hope' its special ring; that is, it is expressed in that ring. – If the feeling gives the word its meaning, then here 'meaning' means *point*. But why is the feeling the point? Is hope a feeling?[3]

That hope is a feeling might seem obvious – we do after all say that we *feel* hopeful – but everyday language doesn't clearly distinguish between what is and what isn't feeling.[4] For example, fear and anger would be paradigmatic examples of feeling, while surprise would be more of a limit phenomenon. In everyday speech it has also become more common to say 'I feel that X', where X is the subject, and the feeling involved must be some kind of sensation or certainty. The term 'feeling' denotes a wide variety of phenomena ranging from pain, hunger and thirst to jealousy, envy and love, the former being more physical and the latter more mental. Some would, by extension, distinguish between 'feelings' and 'emotions', with the former being more physical and the latter more mental, but whether such a distinction can be made especially clearly is debatable. I personally doubt that we can give a good definition that states necessary and sufficient conditions for something to be a feeling.[5]

Some categorize hope as a form of joy, but the two are obviously different. Often a hope will not be felt at all, especially if what we are hoping for is fairly unimportant to us. I can say to a colleague who is going on holiday that I hope he will have good weather on the trip, without becoming in any way emotional, but nevertheless hoping sincerely. Other times a hope can be so emotionally strong that it permeates your entire body, such as when I'm on a knife-edge watching the last balls of a tiebreak in the deciding set of an important tennis tournament, or I'm sitting in the waiting room at the animal hospital while my dog is having surgery. There's no doubt that I can be hopeful without feeling an ounce of joy. For example, I can believe that something has a high likelihood of going really badly and be depressed about it but still hope that things will get better. But I will still be less depressed than if I had thought that all hope was lost.

The Canadian philosopher Katie Stockdale claims that there is also hope that is characterized by negative emotions, specifically what she calls 'fearful hope', which at its core is not about a desire to achieve something positive but rather to escape a threat.[6] An example could be a young woman walking home alone through empty streets in a city where a number of assaults and rapes have recently been committed. She hopes to get home safely but is definitely not in a positive state emotionally. One can always insist that hope is, by definition, characterized by positive emotions and that this woman is simply in a state of fear, not hope. Sometimes it will be unclear to us whether we hope or fear, or do both interchangeably, not least when something that means a lot to us is at stake.

Often there will also be gradual transitions between other emotions, such as fear and anger. When people are asked to look at pictures and determine the emotional state of the people depicted, there is a lot of agreement about who is happy or sad, while there is a lot of disagreement about those who are alternately described as scared, angry, surprised or suspicious.[7] Even when people are asked to assess their own emotional state, there is room for interpretation. Two people who are in the same situation and in the same physical state can identify what they are feeling as fear and anger respectively, depending on their interpretation of the situation. They may both be right. Sometimes we also mistake our own feelings, or at least later come to the conclusion that we misidentified our feelings at a given time.[8] The interpretation of what we were feeling at a given time can change over time because we might see ourselves in a new light and then interpret our reactions in a different way.

It's hard to explain what a feeling actually is, let alone to establish what different ones there are and what sets them apart. But we can highlight some of their typical characteristics. First, they are *subjective* – they are about a subject's response to something. Second, they have an intended object – they are *directed* at something. Third, feelings have *valence* – they are positive or negative. Fourth, many emotions have a relatively short *duration*, and this duration is specifically determined by a change in valence – for example, a shift from the experience of being in a negative state to being in a neutral or positive state. This fourth characteristic has so many exceptions that it perhaps shouldn't be considered a criterion at all. Pain can be chronic; you can be angry or envious of someone for years; and you can be lucky to meet someone you love deeply for the rest of your life. So short duration is only a characteristic of some emotions, such as surprise, and not others.

If we consider hope from its emotional aspect, it is clearly subjective. Two people can be in the same situation and have the same intellectual understanding about the likelihood of a given outcome, yet one of them can be hopeful and the other not, so it is clearly a purely subjective response. The second criterion states that ordinary hope always has an intended object – it is directed. But as we will see in Chapter Ten, we can also talk about fundamental or radical hope that does not have an object. Hope likewise has a valence – it is normally positively charged, although Katie Stockdale's concept of 'fearful hope' may be an example of negatively charged hope. As for the fourth criterion we must say that hope typically persists for a longer period of time than many other emotions. Hope will normally last for a while rather than flaring up momentarily before disappearing as quickly as it came. This is probably not least due to the fact that the object of hope is normally at some faraway point in the future, whereas fear, for example, can be far more momentary when something we consider dangerous appears in our field of experience. Hope must also be described as less intense than most other emotions. If you get scared or angry it is a far more powerful experience than hoping. Hope clearly has an emotional side, but that does not mean it should basically be described as a feeling, because it also involves one's understanding of what can happen and what one wants to happen.

Is Hope Exclusive to Humans?

Hope involves all of man's thoughts and emotions. But can non-human animals hope too? Wittgenstein considers this unlikely; he opens Part II of *Philosophical Investigations* (1953) with this passage:

> One can imagine an animal angry, frightened, un-happy, happy, startled. But hopeful? And why not? A dog believes his master is at the door. But can he also believe his master will come the day after tomorrow? – And what can he not do here? How do I do it – How am I supposed to answer this? Can only those hope who can talk? Only those who have mastered the use of a language. That is to say, the phenomena of hope are modes of this complicated form of life.[9]

What my dog loves more than anything is cheese. She can be lying in another room, beneath several layers of duvets, but the moment I get the cheese out to make myself a sand-wich she will suddenly be right there, looking up at me from the kitchen floor with pleading eyes. Sometimes she gets the cheese, sometimes she doesn't. Mostly she does. It is obvious that she really wants cheese, but can we therefore say that she is *hoping* to get it? If so, we have to ascribe her with an awareness that she might not get cheese, that there is only a possibility she will get it. Having said that, nothing about her behaviour suggest that she has such an awareness. What her behaviour tells me is simply that she wants cheese. If, for the sake of argument, we assume that she is unsure whether she will get cheese, we could perhaps ascribe her with a kind of proto-hope.

Hope stretches over time, and animal time is different from human time. Wittgenstein writes:

> Could someone have a feeling of ardent love or hope for the space of one second – no matter what preceded or followed this second? What is happening now has significance – in these surroundings. The surroundings give it its importance. And the word 'hope' refers to a phenomenon of human life.[10]

A phenomenon like pain does not need such context. We can imagine a pain that cuts through the body for a moment, totally detached from what preceded and followed it. But while pain needs no context, hope does. Hope looks beyond the moment. For example, I can hope that something specific will happen tomorrow. My dog cannot hope for cheese tomorrow, for the simple reason that she has no concept of 'tomorrow'. There is also no reason to believe that the cheese has any place in her imagination until it is taken from the fridge and put on the kitchen counter. The dog's proto-hope is related to what is given to the senses here and now, which is far from what we normally understand hope to be in human life.

Wittgenstein links hope to our ability to speak without explaining what the connection consists of. Only humans possess what we normally understand as language. Animals can communicate but they don't have language.[11] Human capacity for language lets time elapse through our lives in a different way than it does for animals. Our ability to speak gives us a degree of independence in our relationship with the world, because we can replace objects with symbols of those objects.[12] So our imaginary world has a greater scope than any other animal can have, and it also gives our emotions a larger range. Language gives us the ability to represent what is not there, what we lack or miss and want, and it is absolutely crucial for our ability to hope.

The ability to hope is something that develops over time, as does the ability to speak. I would not say that an infant can hope, but I would say so of older children and adults. When do we develop the ability to hope? It's hard to tell. We will always be able to pinpoint the time when a child first uses the expression 'hope', but it would be strange to say: 'today my daughter hoped for the first time.'[13] Hope is something that can only arise in human life after many other abilities have developed. In return it is then so intertwined with these and other abilities that it's hard for us to imagine how they would function without being linked to hope. Wittgenstein writes:

> But how would a human being have to act for us to say of him: he never hopes? The first answer is: I don't know. It would be easier for me to say how a human being would have to act who never yearns for anything, who is never happy about anything, or who is never startled or afraid of anything.[14]

It is not hard to imagine a human that isn't in any obvious state of hope right now, but it is hard to imagine a well-functioning human that doesn't have the ability to hope.

Wittgenstein points out that one can show fear by conveying it with an expression, but that hope cannot be presented like that.[15] What kind of expression would I choose to show hope? Wittgenstein claims that hope is related to faith, which also has no physical expression.[16] It is easy to imagine a person who is never afraid, simply by imagining a person who never exhibits the expression that I associate with being afraid. Of course, fear can sometimes be hidden, but if a person has never shown fear, I would have no reason to ascribe that person with the ability to fear. There is a relatively clear connection between fear as a physical expression and fear as a feeling. For hope, there is no such connection. What is the person who never hopes lacking? A short answer is that the person in question never reaches for the future; they are stuck in a now.

To imagine a person without hope I would have to imagine someone who does not relate to what's possible by wanting one thing rather than another. I would then be unable to understand why that person is acting that way, because they won't seem to have any reason at all to do one thing rather than the other. Such a being would be more alien to me than a dog that cannot hope, since the dog's behaviour is, after all, determined by its preferences. I can understand why a dog behaves the way it does because I can understand its intentions, but a human without hope is more of a mystery. There are people who do not hope, either because they have not yet developed the ability or because they have lost the ability due to a brain injury or similar, but normal adults, who have a capacity for rational agency, can hardly be understood without assuming that they have the ability to hope. What about people who have 'lost hope', who have given up? Such a person normally still has the ability to hope but has lost one or more objects of hope.

In Chapter Ten we will return to how we can understand living without hope.

Hope and Time

In *Faust, Part II* (1832) by German writer and polymath Johann Wolfgang von Goethe, fear and hope are described as the greatest foes of humanity.[17] Both fear and hope can lead our lives astray, but they at least lead us somewhere. A life without fear and hope would be a life where nothing really matters. It would be a life in an almost vegetative state. Then one can argue that a vegetative life might also be attractive. Goethe's friend, the romantic poet, philologist and philosopher Friedrich Schlegel, writes: 'And so the highest, most perfect mode of life would actually be nothing more than pure vegetating.'[18] However, this presumably vegetative state is not without purpose. It is about finding peace in longing and longing in peace.[19] For Schlegel it is love, but it might have been a different goal. By longing for a goal, hope creeps into the picture again. Then one might object to us experiencing moments of happiness where we are fully present here and now, totally content, without a thought aimed at the past or future. Such moments do occur but they are exceptions to an experience of time that stretches backwards and forwards, where the happiness is something we look back on or forward to. The moment does not last, and can never become a permanent present. Even this moment – which might be one of aesthetic bliss at a concert, for example – is what it is because of its relationship to the past and future. If you are immersed in music, you can hear what you are hearing because of all the music you've heard before, and each note you hear is simultaneously a foreshadowing of the next, even if it's a piece of music you've never experienced. The pure now is an abstraction: lived time contains all three dimensions of time.

Hope also contains all three dimensions of time. Your experience of the past tells you what you can hope for in the future, and that in turn tells you how you must behave in the present to help make it come true. Hope is ecstatic – you project yourself into the future. Hope is transcendence, it goes beyond the present. To hope isn't just a state of waiting, sitting back to see what happens, but to be drawn towards the future. It affects my actions because I already – at least partially – behave as if this future were a reality. Our ideas about the future affect our ideas about the present and make us inclined to act in certain ways. Hope is an anticipation. It draws you into an imagined future where what you want is realized. Hope anticipates where an expectation awaits. Hope can have different values, from anxious hope that verges on or is mixed with fear to confident hope that verges on expectation.

The French essayist Michel de Montaigne, among others, warns that hope can make us overlook the present in favour of an imagined future: 'Fear, desire, hope, still push us on towards the future, depriving us, in the meantime, of the sense and consideration of that which is to amuse us with the thought of what shall be, even when we shall be no more.'[20] It is in itself true that we can lose sight of the present by being nostalgic and losing ourselves in a time that has been, or dreaming away in a future that may never come. However, it is too easy to consider past, present and future as three strictly separate axes of time, because what we call the present gets its meaning from what has been and what will be: the past and the future. Montaigne puts it better when he points out that 'without hope and without desire we proceed not worth a pin.'[21] Because what use is anything otherwise?

TWO

Defining Hope

The previous chapter described some of hope's basic characteristics. Now, the question is if the phenomenon can be captured by a definition. But there is no agreement on whether 'hope' can be in any way defined satisfactorily. The problem catches your eye the moment you look a bit closer at the literature in which hope is described as, among other things, a feeling, an emotion, a mood, a state of mind, an activity, a practice, a habit, a disposition, a cognitive process and an existential attitude, and as a combination of all these things. Some regard hope as an anthropological constant, coded into our genetic material, others as a highly changeable social construction. The literature offers a wide variety of theories and definitions. Most of these theories and definitions appear to capture essential aspects of hope. If nothing else, this tells us that hope is a complex phenomenon that will be hard for one theory or definition to capture. Perhaps what we call hope is not one unified phenomenon but several partially overlapping phenomena.

Some philosophers have defined hope as a feeling that things will not necessarily, but most likely, go as one wishes. According to the French philosopher René Descartes, hope is a notion that something will be good for us, but where it is only probable, not certain, that good will be achieved.[1] Precisely because the outcome is uncertain, hope will always be accompanied by fear.[2] Descartes claims that high probability creates the most hope and low probability the most fear, but on that point he is wrong: there can be a very low probability of a desired outcome, but one can still hope for it. The British philosopher Thomas Hobbes writes: 'Appetite with an opinion of attaining, is called hope.'[3] Hobbes seems to think that hope is only possible if one believes that it is most likely that what one is desiring will occur. The British philosopher John Locke defines hope as a sense of desire caused by the idea that one is likely to experience a future pleasure.[4] Locke's philosophical heir, David Hume, also claims that hope requires a preponderance of likelihood. According to Hume, hope is a feeling or, to be more precise, a mixture of pain and pleasure. He writes: ''Tis evident that the very same event, which by its certainty wou'd produce grief or joy, gives always rise to fear or hope, when only probable and uncertain.'[5] The certainty of a good brings pleasure, while the certainty of an evil brings pain. Since hope is linked to uncertainty, it becomes a mixture of the two.

It is no exaggeration to say that these philosophers have a somewhat primitive understanding of hope. Furthermore, as mentioned, the idea is that hope is dependent on you believing something will most likely go as you wish. Suppose a doctor tells me I have a 49 per cent chance of survival and a 51 per cent risk of dying, and that I accept the estimate. There is therefore a slightly higher likelihood of it being the fatal outcome, a situation that – according to Descartes, Hobbes, Locke and Hume's concept of hope – I cannot hope to survive, only fear to die. But I can of course hope, and with far worse odds than that. If the doctor gives me a 99 per cent chance of dying and only a 1 per cent chance of surviving, I can hope to survive. The predominance of likelihood isn't necessary at all, you simply need your wish to not be absolutely impossible. For example, the Austrian psychiatrist Viktor Frankl writes that he assumed there was only a 20 per cent chance of him surviving the three years he spent in concentration camps during the Second World War, but that there was no reason to give up hope, specifically because the future was still open.[6] At the same time, a preponderance of likelihood will not necessarily make you feel hope rather than fear. You might find out that there is a 90 per cent chance of your child surviving an operation and yet be in a state of fear rather than hope, precisely because what is at stake is totally irreplaceable. On the other hand you might be told that there is only a 10 per cent chance of the operation being successful and find that hope is the dominant feeling. The point is that hope and fear are not determined by probability alone.

The so-called orthodox definition of hope states that hope is a combination of wanting a certain outcome and believing that it is possible without being sure of it becoming a reality. Granted, this definition encompasses a great many cases of hope, but it is still unsatisfactory because it partly fails to cover all cases of hope while partly encompassing cases that definitely cannot be described as hope. Furthermore, it is so detached from our actions and deliberations that it does not tell us much about what hope is. Hope is typically related to the power of our imagination, where we imagine the outcome and the possible ways of reaching it, and to a course of action where we do something to realize the desired outcome. Hope is also a motivating force – it often gives us a psychological boost, making us better at coping with adversity. Now a definition doesn't have to cover everything that can be said about a phenomenon, but definitions can sometimes be so thin that they become uninformative.

A problem with the orthodox definition is that it only covers specific hopes and not what I will later call transcendental, fundamental or radical hope, which is precisely characterized by having no object and so cannot be described as a desire for a specific result either. I will not discuss this second form of hope until Chapter Ten, and therefore leave this objection to the orthodox definition for now. As an extension of this objection it can also be pointed out that I can hope for something I only have the vaguest notion of. For example, I believe that virtually every person has a hope of being happy without many of us having a particularly clear idea of exactly what happiness consists of. In that sense, it is problematic to demand that hope requires us to want a certain result when it can be so unclear what that result should actually be.

The definition has other weaknesses too. That there are cases that we would not consider cases of hope, but which satisfy the definition, is at the very least problematic. Let's say that I am a drug addict who wants to kick the habit because I know that it is ruining my whole existence, and I believe that it's possible to become drug-free but am very unsure if I can manage it. This example meets the criteria of the ortho-dox definition, but it could be just as much a description of despair as it is of hope. So my objection is that the definition is incapable of distinguishing between these very heterogeneous phenomena.[7]

Another example could be if you and I were in the stands at Wimbledon on 5 July 1980 watching the final between Björn Borg and John McEnroe. We both want Borg to win his fifth title in a row. He had been in shaky form during the matches prior to the final, but he was still the reigning champion and ranked as the world's best player. McEnroe, for his part, was ranked number two in the world and had performed very convincingly in the matches leading to the final. Before the match things stood at 4–3 to Borg. We agree that it is entirely uncertain which way it will go and determine the likelihood to be 50/50. We therefore have the same desire and the same assessment of the probability. However, throughout the 3 hours and 53 minutes of the match, we are in diametrically opposite states: you are full of hope that Borg will win while I am full of fear that he will lose. This difference between us is something the orthodox definition cannot account for.

Another example could be that you and I each buy a ticket in a lottery that is raising funds for the Cancer Society. Let's further assume that we have an equal desire to win the first prize and that we have the same assessment of our chances of winning. The difference between us is that you are hoping to win, even if you agree that the probability is very low, while I think that the probability is so low that I have no hope of winning – but I do think it's a nice way of contributing to the Cancer Society. Both of us will be satisfying the orthodox definition of hope despite the fact that only one of us can be said to be hoping. It seems that hoping requires more than fulfilling the two criteria. What is the difference between the hopeful and the non-hopeful person? It seems to be linked to one's attitude, one's emotional state, even though hope cannot be reduced to a mere feeling.

Various philosophers and psychologists have tried to improve the orthodox definition by adding new criteria to ensure that the definition is more appropriately limited, in that it better captures the cases that should be considered hope and those that should not.[8] The Belgian philosopher Luc Bovens claims that hope requires 'mental imaging', its premise being that we can say that a person will only hope if they have thought about the object of that hope.[9] For example, if I meet a former colleague at a conference and say that I'd been hoping to meet them there, it would be untrue had I not spared a thought about the possibility of us meeting at said conference. Bovens does not require us to have mental *images* – they can be purely conceptual ideas. It seems fairly obvious that one can only hope if what one is hoping for is in some sense the object of one's conscious thoughts. That rules out 'unconscious hope', should anyone ever want to advocate for it. I wouldn't accept a category like 'unconscious hope' either, but there is undoubtedly a lot of unmathematized hope, that is, hope that is operative in one's actions and consciousness without it explicitly being made the object of one's attention.

For example, I can hope that the bus I want to take will come along – because it is something I expect will happen without having to be certain – but if there were no known problems with public transport, it's not something I would have directed much of my consciousness towards. In my opinion Bovens's 'mental imaging' does not contribute significantly to illuminating the phenomenon of hope.

The Irish philosopher Philip Pettit makes a distinction between superficial and substantial hope and claims that the latter requires cognitive resolve.[10] This means that a person who hopes substantially will at the same time decide to act as if their hope will be fulfilled or is at least most likely to be fulfilled. Pettit accepts the orthodox definition as an analysis of 'superficial' hope, but he believes that it doesn't capture the things that interest us in some important cases of hope, and likewise what makes us ascribe value to it. It's easy to give examples of either: if you buy a lottery ticket without also deciding to act like you want to win, for example, you would be hoping superficially. On the other hand, you would be hoping substantially if you jumped the gun and bought an expensive sports car. Most of our hopes will probably lie somewhere between these extremes, where we act partly as if things are going to turn out as we want and partly as if they are not. Suppose I am diagnosed with a serious illness and I hope to survive despite knowing that the chances of that are fairly poor. In such a situation I can partly fulfil the criterion for substantial hope by planning what I'll be doing with my family when I've recovered – taking great trips to faraway places, for example – but I also cannot meet the criteria because I would act as if things are not going to go my way by making a will and ensuring that my affairs are in order. Would this hope then be considered 'superficial' or 'substantial'? Is a patient's hope less substantial than the sports car buyer's if the patient is also preparing for an unfortunate outcome? Even if you have hope you won't normally want to bet everything on one card but rather plan for an alternative scenario where things don't go as you hope. What Pettit describes is a kind of absolute hope, although we normally have several thoughts in our heads. One could say that the typical hope, at least when something important is at stake, is a partial hope. The person hoping won't normally accept the undesired outcome in advance but will maintain the possibility that things might go well and want to act in a way that might increase the chances of a desirable outcome. A substantial hope, in Pettit's sense, may seem to be more an example of a subjective certainty or expectation than a hope. It seems most reasonable to say that such a cognitive determination can be part of one's hope, provided that the outcome is still only considered a possibility, although it doesn't have to be, and is a dubious basis for distinguishing between distinct types of hope anyway.

The American philosopher Adrienne Martin has what she calls an 'incorporation thesis' of hope, where someone must want X, believe that X has a certain degree of probability, believe that it is rationally acceptable to use the probability assessment as a basis for planning around X and finally believe that the attractive aspects of X are a sufficient reason to hope for X.[11] From an 'incorporation perspective', acting on the basis of a feeling or inclination means that you consider the feeling or inclination a sufficient reason to act. However, the parallel between hope and action fails. To act in a certain way you need to believe that you have sufficient reason to act, but it seems you don't need to believe that you have sufficient reason to hope in order to hope. You can think that your hope is in fact indefensible – for example, because your hope has immoral aspects that you cannot rationally defend – while at the same time acknowledging that you actually have this hope. So hope is more related to other emotions, such as fear, than it is to actions. I can no doubt fear something without then believing that I have valid reason to. Again: a person *can* undoubtedly hope as Martin describes it. I can wish that the soufflé I put in the oven will remain firm and not collapse; I can believe that it's unlikely to collapse, and as I have good reason to believe so, I can plan on serving it to some guests; and finally, I can believe that the soufflé is delicious enough to hope for. We have little reason to believe that people always hope in such an intellectualizing way. Hope doesn't necessarily conform to our rational beliefs: I can believe that X is the most rational but still hope for Y. Or I can hope for X despite knowing that the attractive aspects of X are not sufficient reason to hope for X.

A problem with the most intellectualized theories about hope, such as Martin's, is that they underestimate how much our hopes are also characterized by emotional recalcitrance, in that they don't easily conform to our rational considerations.[12] I can hope for something that I know very well I shouldn't be hoping for. Most of us have presumably found ourselves hoping for something we know isn't good for us and generally don't want to happen. For example, I can fully understand that a girlfriend who has left me wasn't making my life better in any way, and so in that sense I should be extremely happy about her leaving, yet my overriding hope is for her to come back. Such a hope is as real as any hope I give my rational consent to. Of course, what I hope for is something I want, but what I want may be something my reason tells me I shouldn't want.

A drug addict might rifle through all his clothes and drawers hoping to find a forgotten packet of drugs while simultaneously not wanting another dose because his greatest wish is to live drug-free. Such a person will have conflicting first- and second-order preferences, where the first-order preference will be to take more drugs and the second-order preference will be to not do so. In that sense, the person will hope for something he doesn't want to hope for. I might see a neighbour who I don't like that much standing at the top of a slightly unstable ladder repairing a broken gutter: I can then hope that he'll fall and hurt himself while simultaneously not wanting that to happen. Alternatively, you could say that I have conflicting desires in that I both want and do not want him to fall. In that sense, we may have to say that we both hope and do not hope that the neighbour will fall. I can be ashamed of my desires and therefore my hopes too. I can be ashamed of my hope because I hope for something that I don't think I should hope for; for example, if my hope is based on envy. As the French moralist and nobleman François de La Rochefoucauld pointed out: 'We often pride ourselves on even the most criminal passions, but envy is a timid and shame-faced passion we never dare acknowledge.'[13] To hope that something will go wrong because you are envious of someone is so low that you should be ashamed. You really shouldn't be that pathetic. But sometimes that's precisely what you are.

One of the two basic elements in the orthodox definition, that hope must be about something you want, is problematic because our desires can be contradictory: we can both want and not want something at the same time, and we can want to not want something, and so on. The last criterion – that hope must be about something possible but not certain – I find convincing, but, at the same time, it is highly insufficient to distinguish hope from countless other phenomena where a person considers the future to be uncertain but where 'hope' would not be the closest term for describing that person's state of mind.

The orthodox definition also lacks a relationship to our actions. Among others the American psychologist C. R. Snyder emphasizes that to hope is to consider oneself capable of finding possible paths to one's goals, and to follow those paths.[14] From that perspective hope will typically manifest itself in action. Hope will be something you do, and by doing so you will also increase probability. By hoping, you are more likely to achieve what you desire. This is because hope manifests itself as actions that lead you towards the goal, and thus brings you closer to the goal than if you don't hope and don't act. Contrary to Snyder's and others' strong emphasis on hope being an action is the fact that we also hope in contexts where our actions are irrelevant to the outcome, where we can do nothing but observe how things eventually turn out. Suppose we found ourselves in a situation much like the one in Lars von Trier's film *Melancholia* (2011), where a planet called Melancholia is heading towards Earth and will destroy all life here should it hit. As long as there is a possibility of Earth not being affected by this planet, there is hope, although in reality no one can do anything to influence the outcome either way. A less spectacular example could be if I'm told that a close friend or relative has been rushed to hospital and is lying on the operating table, fighting for their life. Of course, I would hope that the operation will be successful even if I cannot influence what happens on the operating table. So I can undoubtedly hope despite the fact that my actions cannot influence the outcome. Not just that: I can also hope for an outcome and in fact be able to contribute to this outcome, albeit marginally, without actually acting. For example, I can hope for a change of government without writing newspaper articles, getting involved politically, making financial donations or, for that matter and for the sake of convenience, even voting, if it's raining on election day. Such a hope cannot be said to run very deep, but it is a hope all the same.

Hope, then, might not end with action, although it often will. Even in the cases where you neither can nor want to contribute with action of your own, your hope is an expression of you being an agent with an interest and readiness for action should the opportunity arise. When hope leads to action, it always contains an insight into the limitations of our agency. If we can easily achieve our desires, with no internal or external obstacles, there is no room for hope. Hope implies an awareness that our goal will not necessarily be realized, regardless of how much effort we put into it. We are limited beings, and by hoping we attempt to manage these limitations. Hope gives us a direction, an experience of having a certain measure of control because it gives the future a structure within all the uncertainty. It thereby also helps us to persevere when life goes against us.

The American philosopher Margaret Urban Walker refers to hope as a 'syndrome' – that is, a complex phenomenon containing a variety of feelings, dispositions, thoughts, actions and so on – and claims that trying to narrow it down to the lowest common denominator is futile.[15] It is instead more appropriate to approach hope via what Wittgenstein calls family resemblances. Wittgenstein illustrates this using the term 'games': none of these games shares any single characteristic, but they are nevertheless all connected through a network of similarities.[16] A consequence of a Wittgensteinian approach to the term 'hope' is that one must consider it through the use of examples. We can give examples of something we call hope, as well as examples of what we do not want to call hope, but we neither can nor must state a definition with necessary and sufficient conditions. Hope is difficult to understand in isolation and must be seen in relation to countless other aspects of human life.

THREE

Is Hope Irrational?

To hope might immediately seem irrational because it involves putting one's trust in something that is highly uncertain while knowing that it is uncertain. Wouldn't a more rational approach to life be to instead base your expectations on things that are certain, and take any good outcomes beyond that purely as a bonus? That might seem to be the case, but it might also be possible that hope itself makes a better outcome more likely than certainty alone.

Nietzsche's Scepticism towards Hope

As we have seen Nietzsche is definitely sceptical of hope when he comments on the myth of Pandora, claiming that hope is the greatest of all evils because it prolongs human suffering. He is particularly sceptical of those who link hope to the hereafter. Such a hope requires people to live in an illusion; it is a hope that can neither be disproved nor made superfluous by being fulfilled, precisely because it will never be fulfilled in our earthly life:

> Strong hope is a much greater stimulus to life than any piece of individual happiness that actually falls our way. Suffering people need to be sustained by a hope that cannot be refuted by any reality – that is not *removed* by any fulfilment: hope for a beyond.[1]

Nietzsche is also highly critical of hope linked to the worldly and claims, among other things, that the state, not least through the school system, indoctrinates young people into getting a range of ideas about how they should live, such as having a career and a family, which constitutes 'a net of expectations within which every young man is caught'.[2] He is also sceptical of 'the Socialist pied-pipers whose design is to enflame you with wild hopes' that they must wait to have fulfilled by forces outside themselves.[3] Hope makes one passive; it is the real 'opium of the people', to use an expression from Marx. The Greek Stoic Epictetus is highlighted as an ideal: he was self-sufficient precisely because he did not hope for anything.[4] Epictetus' life advice was that one should not strive to make things happen as one wishes but rather wish that they happen exactly as they happen.[5]

At the same time, we do find some positive remarks about hope in Nietzsche's writings. For example, he links hope to a change in society that results from a new understanding of human life:

> Our social order will slowly melt away, as all previous orders have done, as soon as the suns of novel opinions shine out over mankind with a new heat. One can *desire* this melting away only if one harbours hope: and one may reasonably harbour hope only if one credits oneself and one's kind with more power in head and heart than is possessed by the representatives of what at present exists. Usually, therefore, this hope will be a piece of *presumption* and an *overvaluation*.[6]

Hope can only be justified if there is reason to believe that it can be fulfilled. Unfortunately, it can only be fulfilled if there are 'new people' of a different calibre to those who have hitherto inhabited the modern world. Furthermore, Nietzsche seems to think that we easily go from hoping to believing that the hope is justified, that we believe we can change the world only because we hope that we can, and this implies a misjudgement: we overestimate ourselves. Hope then makes us conceited. It becomes nothing more than wishful thinking. Nietzsche claims that the philosophers' 'family failing' is that they use today's human as a basis and then believe they can reach their goal by analysing it.[7] Instead, hope must be linked to a future man who is of a different cast to today's version. He suggests that this man could be 'a few thousand years' in the future, but that in return he might 'feel entitled to venture to harbour even greater expectations'.[8] Nietzsche hopes that in the future it will be possible to access greater hope than contemporary man is able to imagine.

Nietzsche, therefore – unlike Arthur Schopenhauer, who had previously been his philosophical role model – is receptive to hope. However, it is not a hope for us ordinary people. For us, it is irrational to hope. The greatest thing we can achieve is to accept fate, or rather to embrace and love fate:

> My formula for human greatness is *amor fati*: that you do not want anything to be different, not forwards, not backwards, not for all eternity. Not just to tolerate necessity, still less to conceal it – all idealism is hypocrisy towards necessity – but to love it.[9]

The idea is to make oneself invulnerable: '*necessity* does not hurt me; *amor fati* is my innermost nature.'[10] But through this Nietzsche seems to fall back into the position for which he rightly criticizes the Stoics. The mistake of the Stoics was to eliminate desire in order to avoid undesire.[11] The Stoic is someone who 'trains himself to swallow stones and worms, glass shards and scorpions without nausea; he wants his stomach to be ultimately insensible to everything the chance of existence pours into him.'[12] Although life undoubtedly puts us to the test, it's really not so bad that we need to become Stoics, remarks Nietzsche.[13] We should get more out of life than stoicism allows. Whoever loves fate must also love the pain that is part of this fate, Nietzsche claims, while the Stoic tries to shield himself entirely from pain. Sometimes Nietzsche seems to fetishize pain, such as when he writes about a 'thirst for pain', but his point is that pain is inevitable for those who should also be able to experience joy.[14]

The Benefits of Hope

The Romanian philosopher E. M. Cioran believed that to hope is to blind oneself to life as it really is because one is indulging in an illusion. Hope characterizes the weak who are unable to internalize true pessimism: 'One is and remains a slave as long as one is not cured of hoping.'[15] But what exactly is one freed to do if one manages to be cured? For Cioran hope makes one passive – it turns life into an eternal waiting process.[16] Hope can be like that, but it doesn't have to be. There is also an active hope. Moreover, it is hard to think of anything more passive than being without hope. Cioran writes in *On the Heights of Despair* (1992) that he is in a state without hope, where everything that can make life attractive is meaningless, where he feels nothing for the future or the past, while the present seems toxic, where he feels that there is nothing for him to lose because he has lost everything and is primarily distant from everything.[17] One might ask: would he even be able to write those lines if he were in the condition he describes? Probably not, because in such a state he wouldn't even bother to write. In this sense, we could say that although Cioran is right, that hope can make you passive, nothing can make you more passive than hopelessness.

The American law professor William Ian Miller is a generally wise and funny writer, albeit one with a consider- ably dark view that has darkened with each book. He has few positive things to say about hope, which he considers no more than a form of irrationality that accompanies one's own misery. Instead, he highlights the phenomenon of luck. The sense of having been lucky creates gratitude. It is a retrospective feeling because the answer is available and you can breathe a sigh of relief. Both small and large hopes usually end in disappointment, so you should forget about hope and instead be grateful on the rare occasions you are lucky, claims Miller.[18] That's bad advice.

A standard argument against hoping is that if you don't hope, you won't be disappointed if things don't work out, but you can still be fully satisfied if things do. By not hoping, you eliminate the risk of disappointment while maintaining the possibility of benefitting. This argument is based on the assumption that the likelihood of achieving X is not affected by whether one hopes for X. Such an assumption is dubious because it views hope as being detached from our actions when in many cases hoping for X will promote actions that increase the likelihood of X being achieved. How hopeful an individual is becomes a strong predictor of how well this individual will succeed in realizing life goals, such as having well-functioning relationships, mastering an education and a professional life, finding life meaningful and so on. Hopeful people also experience setbacks and failure and suffer accidents and tragedy, but the likelihood of achieving what you want in life is far greater if you are hopeful than if you are not.[19]

There will also be occasions where my actions cannot influence the outcome, in which case the argument might seem more convincing. The explanation, however, is more complicated than the sceptic might assume. In hope, you take some of the joy in advance and it's not obvious if this joy is smaller than the disappointment when things don't go the way you wanted. Hope can also provide comfort if the outlook is really bad.

When my father got cancer, what kept him going was hope. I accompanied him to the doctor's appointment at

Oslo University Hospital when he was given the discouraging diagnosis. The likelihood of surviving oesophageal cancer is small and the course of the disease unattractive, to put it mildly. The doctor who delivered the message was keen to avoid creating false hope, but the problem was that he left no room for hope whatsoever. Fortunately, my father got a new doctor who certainly didn't gloss over the situation, but he did point out the possibilities that existed. He gave my father a task: to stay in shape, as well as possible, so that he would be able to withstand a very extensive operation and after that operation get back in shape. The disease's course was complicated and a year and a half later he died – not from the tumour in the oesophagus itself, but from it spreading to other organs. We can say that he lived one year in hope and then half a year in acceptance that there was no longer any basis for hope. Or more correctly: when all hope of getting better was gone, it was replaced with a new hope that the disease would follow the best possible course until it was over. And that was something he got, to a fair degree. Of course, when it became clear that no more could be done, that the hope of becoming cancer-free was lost, the disappointment was enormous, but there is no doubt that until that point the hope had made his existence significantly better as the illness had progressed. Upon learning that the cancer had spread, he quickly changed from hope to acceptance. As far as quality of life goes, I think we can safely say that he got a better life from a year of hope and six months of acceptance than he would have got from a year and a half of just acceptance.

The cancer-stricken American author Barbara Ehrenreich wrote: 'I hate hope.'[20] I can understand that since she had been bombarded with a form of positive psychology that didn't allow her to feel that life was crap when in fact that was exactly what she felt. She felt under pressure to deny the seriousness of the situation she found herself in. Instead, she advocated for living free of hope, which meant acknowledging the reality of having cancer and then planning her life accordingly. However, this is a false opposition between hope and realism. Those who hope well are precisely those who understand and acknowledge the state of things while stressing that the future is not yet closed.

Hope and Self-Deception

Hope can also be an expression of self-deception that will typically be linked to the likelihood of what you want to happen. Perhaps we hope because we are victims of self-deception but also become victims of self-deception because we hope. In philosophy self-deception is a hotly-debated topic and some philosophers deny that the phenomenon exists at all. Personally I think the British philosopher Bernard Williams offers a plausible account of the phenomenon. He claims that the self-deceiver does not fail himself in order to be honest, because the self-deceiver actually believes in the perception he deceives himself with, and that the failure instead lies in a lack of accuracy. The self-deceiver is sincere, but he fails to make sure that this sincerity is built on stable foundations. As he writes: 'our failures as self-deceived are to be found more significantly, in fact, in our lack of epistemic prudence as victims than in our insincerity as perpetrators.'[21] When you want something to be true you don't absorb information that suggests that it actually isn't true. We all have a confirmation bias, which means that we have a tendency to look for confirmation of what we already believe to be true, and we are not especially open to the fact that there is valuable information that contradicts our existing beliefs. When you have hope you look for confirmation that your hope is justified and ignore information that suggests the outlook is worse. If you're going to hope well you have to hope realistically, and that depends on you being able to fight your own confirmation bias.

For a philosopher like Arthur Schopenhauer, who we will return to in detail in Chapter Nine, hope is little more than a self-delusion of which we should try to rid ourselves. Hope as such does not amount to self-deception at all. It only becomes self-deception when we, in one way or another – despite our better judgement and despite there being information we have good reason to trust – consider something impossible to be possible, or dramatically overestimate the probability of a desired outcome. We have no reason to believe that most hopes are of this kind. Most of the time they are rationally justifiable, although it must be admitted that most of us have a rather poor understanding of probability.

For example, if there is a lengthy drought there is nothing irrational about wanting it to rain. On the contrary, it is the only reasonable thing to want. Nor is it irrational to hope for rain even when most people are saying that the drought will last for a long time. The irrational thing would be to believe it will start raining because one wanted it to, that my wanting it could in itself cause a change in the external world. Wittgenstein wrote a comprehensive critique of the Scottish anthropologist J. G. Frazer's masterpiece *The Golden Bough* (1890), a comparative study of religion and mythology. One of Wittgenstein's main objections was that Frazer ascribes the natives he discusses with irrational beliefs for which there is no evidence: for example, that a certain ritual will make it rain. The problem is that Frazer is unable to see what the natives are actually doing. Wittgenstein states: 'Frazer is much more savage than most of his savages . . . His explanations of primitive practices are much cruder than the meaning of these practices themselves.'[22] While Frazer believes that the natives' actions are based on mistaken beliefs about causal relationships, Wittgenstein suggests that they are not based on such beliefs at all.[23]

Once, after a very bad game, I smashed my tennis racket. Had my opponent thought like Frazer, he would have believed that my action was a ritual sacrifice aimed at changing the outcome of the tournament for me. But my action was not based on any such expectation. It was simply an immature expression of anger and disappointment. The most reasonable understanding of the natives' ritual practices involves considering them as expressions of hope, among other things, not as irrational notions of causal relationships. Our idea of causation stems from us observing regularities.[24] We will have repeatedly seen that A is followed by B. What regularities would have led the natives to see a causal relationship between a specific ritual and a specific natural phenomenon such as rain? It is unlikely that rain was usually brought about by a specific dance, and the natives must have seen that it sometimes rains despite no ritual being performed. Not least, the natives should have danced a lot during the driest parts of the year, but they didn't. So it's far more plausible to consider this dance an expression of *hoping* for rain. From that perspective there is nothing irrational about the natives' actions. The dancing is a shared expression of their understanding that the desired rain might come.

Hope, as Such, Is Neither Rational Nor Irrational

The British philosopher John Stuart Mill writes that a hopeful attitude to the world spurs our faculties and keeps them in good working order.[25] David Hume, for his part, expresses scepticism about hope precisely because it leads to what he calls 'enthusiasm'.[26] Since the word 'enthusiasm' is today positively charged it seems strange to us that it would be used as an argument against hope, but what Hume means by enthusiasm is a kind of religious madness – by no means something of which he approves. On the other hand he also writes that a propensity to hope and feel joy is one of life's riches.[27] Hope can enrich life, but it can also lead to irrationality.

My hope can, of course, be irrational, but it is not an irrationality that is attached to hope as such. With absolutely everything that involves beliefs I can misstep and fall into irrationality. Whether a specific hope should be described as rational or irrational depends entirely on how one is hoping. A large part of hope is also non-rational – that is, neither rational nor irrational. Two people can have exactly the same assessment of the likelihood of an outcome they both want equally. In other words they are equal in terms of rationality; however, one of them can still hope while the other doesn't, as we saw in the example of the two spectators watching the Borg and McEnroe tennis match.

Some describe hope as a virtue. Virtues are character traits that make you function well as a person. Hope doesn't necessarily do that. You cannot function well without hope, but you don't necessarily function well *with* hope because you can hope badly. Virtue is about doing well as a human being. And one can argue that you cannot do well as a human being without hope. On the other hand one can hope in a way that falls short. Hope doesn't conform to our rationality just like that. What I hope for will depend on what I want. I might want something that I know isn't good for me or something that my reason tells me is worthless. I will not draw as sharp a distinction as Hume, who said: 'Reason is, and ought only to be the slave of the passions, and can never pretend to any other office than to serve and obey them.'[28] Without me going into detail here it seems clear that rational considerations play a role in what and how I desire, but desire also has its own logic that doesn't readily conform to reason.

Hope will have reasons. Hope can be more or less justi-fied. Those who hope can be so out of touch with reality that their hoping is little more than wishful thinking or escapism. However, it is not irrational to hope if your hope contains a reasonable understanding of the likelihood of success. Hoping well demands more than having a realistic understanding of the likelihood that what you want will come true. You must also have patience, because it can take time; it can require endurance, because the road ahead can be difficult; it can require courage, because the road is dangerous; and so on. In short, hope cannot be understood independent of many other qualities. In order to hope rationally you must at least hope for something worth hoping for.

FOUR

Hope and Freedom

Hope takes place in the domain of the possible. To hope for something it must be possible for one thing or the other to happen. If the world is governed by a strict necessity, there is little room for hope, beyond any that would be due to my ignorance of the final outcome. A more substantial hope must be linked to my ability to influence the outcome, to the fact that I can help create one future rather than another.

Spinoza: Insight into Necessity Is Freedom

The Dutch philosopher Baruch Spinoza aims to show us how to live a happy life, but he makes it clear that hope is not a part of this happy life because such a life must be rational, and hope will always be an expression of irrationality. He believes such irrationality will also make us unfree. In his early work, *Short Treatise on God, Man and His Well-Being* (*c.* 1660), Spinoza devotes a chapter to fear and hope where he defines hope as a joy in the soul brought about by the idea of a future good that may occur, but adds that this joy will always be mingled with some sorrow.[1] If, however, one goes from hoping to being certain that a future good will occur, there will be no sorrow. Emotions are vague representations for Spinoza, and to indulge in them would be to indulge in irrationality. Spinoza is dismissive about hope because it is based on a misguided view of the world. Hope is linked specifically to the fact that one thing or the other can happen, while Spinoza claims that whoever has genuine insight knows that every event happens with necessity: the future is just as determined as the past.

Spinoza's view of hope in this early work is close to that which he develops with greater precision in *Ethics* (1677), where he describes hope as a form of joy, albeit an unstable one; an 'inconstant pleasure, arising from the image of a thing future or past, of whose outcome we are in doubt'.[2] For Spinoza this hope is irrational because we tend to hope more than we fear, and this leads us to overestimate or underestimate the likelihood of some event and become superstitious.[3] Moreover, hope is always combined with fear and this in itself implies that we cannot regard hope as entirely good. At the same time it must be stressed that for Spinoza hope is a variant of joy, and thus something that increases your power, while fear is a variant of sadness, and thus something that weakens it. Hope is equally a sign of a person's lack of insight into the world's nature, and one should try to free oneself from the powerlessness that hope expresses and instead be guided by reason: 'Therefore the more we endeavor to live by the guidance of reason, the more we endeavor to be independent of hope, to free ourselves from fear, and to command fortune as far as we can, and to direct our actions by the sure counsel of reason.'[4]

Spinoza claims that we are subject to the laws of nature, and our emotions follow these laws. We cannot wipe out our emotions, but we can learn to understand why we feel the way we do and thereby achieve a degree of freedom from the rule of emotions. Spinoza's world is thoroughly determined, and not just physically. For example, when billiard ball B rolls away because it is struck by billiard ball A, our thoughts are determined in the same way, coming one after the other. The individual person is something tiny that basically disappears in the larger context, a context characterized by an unrelenting causal necessity. Man is abandoned to external circumstances, like a rubber ball constantly bumping into its surroundings without being able to control where it will end up.

Nevertheless, Spinoza's principal work is called *Ethics*, and ethics is related to human actions. So what determines human actions according to Spinoza? It is not reason or moral consideration but something he calls 'affects'. Man has three basic affects, namely desire, joy and sorrow. All other affects are derived from these. There's no sense in describing these affects and actions as good or evil because they happen out of necessity. According to Spinoza, when we use the words 'good' and 'evil' for actions, we simply mean that the actions we call good are useful to us, while those we call evil are not. The last part of *Ethics* is a study of freedom and happiness, and that might seem strange in a worldview where everything happens out of necessity. The answer lies in the fact that the affects are not just bodily states, they are representations of these states. By acknowledging the affects, man will gain insight into his own nature, and through this he can become free.

For Spinoza freedom isn't free will or the absence of natural necessity, but self-determination. If you are determined by yourself you are not forced to do anything by external factors. Freedom thus arises from no longer being determined by something external to yourself. We can gain freedom only to the degree that we can gain insight into the laws that govern all life. Because freedom is not about overcoming these laws but following them voluntarily, this can only be done to the extent that one knows them. If I acknowledge that these laws are part of my nature, I will not suffer from them either. I will then learn to love my fate: *amor fati*. And if I love my fate, because I understand out of reason that nothing can be different from what it is, it makes hope totally superfluous. As we shall find in the next chapter, however, Spinoza considers this quite differently when he considers man as a political being.

Hope Presupposes Freedom

As Spinoza sees it I can only be free by freeing myself from hope and accepting necessity. I would say the opposite: hope and freedom are inextricably linked. We only have a capacity for freedom where there is room for genuine hope, but, conversely, hope can promote our capacity for freedom by opening the world to us as a field of possibilities. None of us are infallible, all-knowing or all-powerful. That is why there can be hope. My knowledge of causal relationships is inadequate, and my ability to produce the effects I want is extremely limited. The perspectives I have on any phenomenon, let alone the totality of all phenomena, will never amount to more than a sliver of the truth. Furthermore, I am not entirely transparent to myself; I can never say with total certainty why I act the way I do. Nevertheless, I must act. We can say that any action takes place on inadequate grounds. Our finitude, the fact that we are limited beings who live a life with a beginning and an end, is an unvarying prerequisite for hope, both for hope to exist at all and for how far hope should reach. However, there are also limits to my limitation. I have a certain amount of control and I can have a better or worse base of knowledge when I act. I am not entirely at the mercy of my surroundings.

I have the ability to act freely, but this freedom will always be limited.[5] The limitations of freedom are not uniform. Some limitations are absolute, such as how the laws of physics put limits on what my body can do, while other limitations are changeable through social or personal processes. Some limitations are morally and politically legitimate, while others are not. Either way, it is a fact that the world does not readily conform to my wishes and this is precisely what allows for hope. The term 'freedom' has a wide variety of meanings; however, a kind of minimum requirement that most people should be able to agree on is that freedom must at least include the possibility of living one kind of life rather than another, of shaping one's life. But since we are finite beings this will take the form of *hoping* for one kind of life rather than another.

What is the opposite of hope? Several candidates come to mind: fear, despair and apathy. Fear and hope are symmetrically related in that one imagines a future situation to be avoided, while the other imagines a situation to be achieved, but in both of these cases the outcome is uncertain. Despair, on the other hand, is characterized by certainty that something important has fallen apart, or is going to – in despair, there is no possibility for things to go well. Apathy is a state beyond despair where one is not even interested in what could have been. Both fear and hope have an open future, while the future of despair and apathy is closed. That is why the poor people who find themselves in Hell in the Italian poet Dante Alighieri's *Divine Comedy* can neither hope nor fear, only despair. Above the gate to Hell it says that those who pass through must abandon all hope. It could also say that they must abandon all fear. As the medieval philosopher Thomas Aquinas pointed out: 'Fear is never without some hope of escape: and the lost have no such hope. Consequently neither will there be fear in them; except speaking in a general way, in so far as any expectation of future evil is called fear.'[6] The damned will spend eternity in exactly the situation they are in. There is no possibility for them to do better or worse. One can hope and fear in purgatory but not in Hell or paradise. As Dante sees it hope isn't just about feeling something detached from the reasons you have for feeling it. When you arrive in Hell you must abandon all hope because any reason you might have to be hopeful will be destroyed there. You can only hope if it is possible that what you are wishing for will be fulfilled. This possibility does not exist in Hell.

The German American philosopher Hannah Arendt links the possibility of hope to natality, to the fact that people are born, since every birth is the beginning of something new.[7] Every birth shows us that the future is open. Or does it? The

French mathematician and physicist Pierre-Simon Laplace created a thought experiment concerning a demon who knew everything about the position and momentum of every object in the world and all the laws of nature. This enabled the demon to predict any future event and every human action. Within such a model there is total symmetry between past and future in the sense that the future is as determined as the past: there is only one possibility. As the American pragmatist William James put it: 'Possibilities that fail to get realised are, for determinism, pure illusions; they never were possibilities at all.'[8] Laplace's demon would be unable to feel hope specifically because the future is entirely predetermined. From the demon's perspective, what will happen in the future would be absolutely certain and therefore offer no room for hoping for one outcome rather than the other. Hope presupposes an open future.

A hard determinist might say:

> What happens, happens by necessity. There is no such thing as free will. There is only one possible future, and nothing I do can change that future. Nevertheless, there is room for hope because my knowledge of the causal relationships that produce this future is so limited that I cannot be certain what the future holds. In other words, I can hope for a good rather than a bad future, and that distinguishes me from Laplace's demon.

The hard determinist is correct in thinking that this is a kind of hope, but it is a poor hope since it is detached from everything he could think of doing to create a better future.

The Calvinist, as depicted by the German sociologist Max Weber, becomes a theological-determinist example of such a position.[9] The Calvinist lives in a universe where the only thing that essentially matters is whether or not one achieves heavenly salvation. What material goods one can acquire, for example, is irrelevant. The only thing that counts is salvation, but there is absolutely nothing the individual can do to influence whether or not salvation will be his. A few lucky chosen ones are destined to be saved, while everyone else is not, and there is nothing – no good deeds or intentions – that can affect the individual's final outcome. In that sense whether you live a virtuous or sinful life is irrelevant. If you're chosen, you're chosen, and if you're not chosen, you're not. Your destiny has been totally predetermined regardless of whether you have chosen to live a virtuous or sinful life. The great mystery, then, is why the Calvinist does his utmost to live a virtuous life in which the deprivations are many and the work is hard. He gains nothing from this effort, which is understood to be something that might change the outcome of the only thing that matters. Weber claims that the Calvinist is fully aware of this; the outcome cannot be changed. However, the Calvinist thinks that God will have probably chosen those individuals who to the largest degree embody his ideals, and the closer the Calvinist is to those ideals, the more reason he will have to believe that he is one of those who has been chosen. If you are managing to live as virtuous a life as possible you will be able to interpret this as a sign that you are one of God's chosen ones.

If determinism is correct there is only room for a hope that comes from ignorance about the future. The future is then what it is – as predetermined as the past – but our lack of insight allows for a hope that it may develop one way rather than the other. For a more substantial hope – one where we are not at the mercy of having to wait for the outcome of history but can instead help to increase the likelihood that the object of hope is realized – determinism must be incorrect. Do we have reason to believe that determinism provides a correct description of the world in that only one outcome is ever possible? In most sciences we only manage to predict events with a degree of probability, but the accuracy will vary. Based on what we know today we have no grounds for saying that only one future is possible, so general determinism lacks a scientific foundation. Most of the reasons we draw into scientific explanations involve probability. In other words a given cause makes it more *likely* that something will happen, which is different from something inevitably happening. Sometimes it will only increase the probability a little, other times a lot. And sometimes a given cause will have an inevitable effect. Nevertheless, despite what we think we know about causality there is little reason to assume that we are living in a universe ruled by strict necessity. We live in a universe where it is entirely reasonable to claim that the future is open, that it can play out one way or the other. We live in a universe with room for substantial hope. Every moment of your life is subjected to an infinite number of different causes, from the smallest elementary particles to world politics. We are all, as one, participants within a causal field that gives us room for agency. This room can be large or small, and a political goal must be to increase the room for agency for as many people as possible. In short: to create more room for hope.[10]

Hobbes points out that hope plays a role in our deliberations on how we should act since our judgements can waver according to which hope or fear applies most.[11] He refers to hope as 'honourable' because it springs from the awareness of power.[12] By that we mean power over one's own situation. With hope, you do not see yourself as entirely at the mercy of your circumstances. Hope is liberating – but only partially, because with hope you always have one foot in the present and one in the future. Hope can be part of our freedom because it enhances our ability to create the future we want.

FIVE

The Politics of Hope

Discouraging as it may be for us philosophers, we can safely say that people's political convictions are based less on philosophical theories than they are on fears and hopes. Whether hope or fear motivates us politically makes a difference because only a society based on hope rather than fear will be capable of being free. At the same time it is crucial that political hope is kept in check, not least that it accepts people as they are instead of presupposing a complete transformation of human nature. Utopian hopes that leave no room for anything but model citizens are recipes for political disasters.

Spinoza and the Inevitability of Political Hope

As we saw in the previous chapter, Spinoza claims that indulging in hope is irrational because hope is contingent on an illusory freedom. A true wise man, one who allows himself to be guided entirely by his reason, will not succumb to hope – or be moved by fear – as Spinoza sees it, but it is a fact that few, if any, embody this ideal completely. In reality, all of us will be far more influenced by our emotions than Spinoza's idealized wise man, and most of us are quite a long way from the ideal. A sound political philosophy must be based on people as they actually are, not as one would like them to be.[1] Spinoza opens his *Theological-Political Treatise* (1670) by lamenting how people are normally dependent on hope and fear because they are unable to fully reach a rational understanding of their life circumstances:

> If men were always able to regulate their affairs with sure judgment, or if fortune always smiled upon them, they would not get caught up in any superstition. But since people are often reduced to such desperate straits that they cannot arrive at any solid judgment and as the good things of fortune for which they have a boundless desire are quite uncertain, they fluctuate wretchedly between hope and fear. This is why most people are quite ready to believe anything. When the mind is in a state of doubt, the slightest impulse can easily steer it in any direction, and all the more readily when it is hovering between hope and fear, though it may be confident, pompous and proud enough at other times.[2]

Here hope should only be regarded as a form of irrationality that leads us astray, in full accordance with what Spinoza writes in *Ethics*. Hope is a source of superstition, on an equal footing with hatred, anger and deceit, he writes.[3] However, we see that when Spinoza has to explain how the liberal society he wants can be realized, he cannot avoid hope. Not only that: people who neither fear anything nor hope for anything have so much power over themselves that they are enemies of the State, against whom the State must ultimately use force, he claims.[4] Since the person who has reached an adequate insight – that is, the philosopher – specifically refuses to be led by hope and fear, it seems to follow that the philosopher is an enemy of the State, even if that's not how Spinoza formulates it.

In *Ethics*, Spinoza writes that although the true purpose of the State is to ensure our freedom and security, and democracy is the most natural form of government for a State, the hoi polloi are dangerous if they are not governed by fear: 'The mob is fearsome, if it does not fear.'[5] In his political treatise he approaches the matter in a fundamentally different way, for example writing that state laws should be designed such that 'people are restrained less by fear than hope of something good which they very much desire.'[6] In this way, citizens will perform their duties willingly. This is to be understood as a criticism of Thomas Hobbes. Spinoza agrees with Hobbes that only feelings of fear or hope can convince people to respect the social contract. According to Hobbes, someone who acts out of fear is as free as someone who acts out of hope. Freedom can only be understood as the absence of obstacles to setting the body in motion.[7] To be free is to act as you wish, and to avoid something because you fear it is to be just as free as when doing something because you want or hope to. Hobbes lays down the principle of 'the silence of the law': anything that is not explicitly forbidden is permitted.[8] When the law is not silent, it roars. The law must create fear, and Hobbes stresses that nothing makes citizens less inclined to break the law than fear.[9] Admittedly he names hope as one of the emotions that can promote peace and order, but he has far greater faith in fear. The State threatens a punishment that exceeds what can be accomplished by violating the rights of other people, and the fear of this punishment is what ensures citizens live together peacefully. This regime of fear is regarded as a free society by Hobbes. Spinoza sees the exact opposite: a regime of fear like this will inevitably create unfree citizens. Only hope can form the basis for a free society.

In Spinoza's political philosophy, hope becomes a resource that he cannot do without. Feelings such as fear and hope offer inadequate cognition, but they are what most people are motivated by and should therefore create the foundation for social order. When Spinoza turns away from fear and towards hope, it is paradoxically enough because fear creates hope. The trouble is that fear promotes the wrong kind of hope. Frightened people will look for something to hope for, but they will hope irrationally and become easy prey for political leaders who are able to mobilize this fear. By scaring the population these leaders can portray themselves as saviours: the only things standing between the citizens and the abyss. If the population allows itself to be manipulated in this manner there are almost no limits to what it can accept and maintain as true and good from its leader. It becomes politically irrational and unfree. When Spinoza emphasizes that security (*securitas*) is one of the State's most important tasks, he is referring to not only physical security but psychological security: freedom from fear. A State that gives itself legitimacy and secures the obedience of its citizens through fear is undermining democracy because the strategy of fear undermines the freedom that is at the core of democracy.

The State that Spinoza advocates for should be based more on hope than fear since only hope is compatible with living in freedom:

> For a free multitude is guided by hope more than by fear, whereas a multitude which has been subjugated is guided more by fear than by hope. The first want to cultivate life; the second care only to avoid death. The first are eager to live for themselves; the second are forced to belong to the victor. So we say that the second are slaves, and the first free.[10]

As Spinoza sees it, hopeful citizens will preserve the State's laws and institutions better than fearful citizens. Hope will create a more reliable and stable State power. The feelings of fear and hope are not just something that the individual has but rather unifying emotions. Spinoza therefore writes about 'a common hope, or fear'.[11] He does not go into significant detail about this common hope, but we can at least envision the two dimensions of political hope: it is constitutive for a political community, because we gather around what we hope for; and it plays an instrumental role in that it increases the likelihood of achieving specific political goals, because we are pulling in the same direction. Citizens cooperate with each other and with the authorities because they hope it will be to their advantage.[12] They could also be pressured into cooperating for fear of sanctions, but hope is preferable since it expresses the citizens' own will and consequently their freedom as well.

Hope and Utopia

The political culture of hope that Spinoza writes about could also be called a culture of trust. There has scarcely been a less trusting society than the Soviet Union in the 1930s.[13] Nobody trusted one another, not even close family members.[14] Anyone was a potential informant for the secret police, so you always had to show that you were a good citizen, loyal to the regime. As Hannah Arendt pointed out, because citizens had to show that they could be trusted by the regime, they could not trust each other.[15] They had to be particularly careful about how they worded things, even in innocent situations, and how they expressed feelings. You could not show that you fell short of the norm for an ideal citizen in any way. Although Soviet Communism was officially devoted to creating a brave new world, and could thus be considered a political project of hope, in reality it was mostly a political culture of fear. Hobbes rather than Spinoza was the norm.

The communist Soviet Union was a utopia that turned out to be a dystopia. The utopian hopes for both too much and too little. He hopes too little for this world and too much for the wonderful new world that is to be realized. Other than pure pessimists and optimists, who believe that things must either go really badly or really well, everyone hopes for a better world. Why not wish for the best possible – or rather, perfect – world? A genuinely utopian project assumes that a new world can only be created after the destruction of the old one. For utopia to be perfect, it cannot contain any remnants of the corrupt old world it looks to replace. 'Utopia' literally means a 'no place', but it is often perceived as a 'good place', that is, a 'eutopia' (after the Greek prefix *eu*, which means 'good', and *topos*, which means 'place').

A utopian hopes for too much and is willing to do too much to see their hope become a reality. Hope without moderation is a recipe for political disaster. Political utopias have some curious similarities. The most striking thing is that they are not made up of people like us. Hardly anyone gets ill. Criminals are a thing of the past. People don't lie, and they certainly don't deceive each other. Utopia has no room for people who are not perfect embodiments of the highest ideals. In short, there is no room for imperfect people like us. This was clearly demonstrated in the Soviet Union, especially under Stalin, where it was assumed that there could be nothing wrong with the utopia itself, and when the brave new world nevertheless failed to become a reality, it had to be because they failed to cleanse the utopia of the people who didn't fit in and who consequently undermined it.[16] This applied especially to people from the lower class. The utopian hopes for too little because he sees no possibility to make different improvements to the society we actually live in. The existing society is perceived as being in such an unacceptable condition that it cannot be saved by gradual improvements. The old has to be eliminated to make way for the new. Reality as we know it is without hope, and everything must be melted down and cast in a new form.

The Liberalism of Hope and Fear

Liberal democracy must be built on hope, but it is not utopian. I place my trust more in the 'liberalism of hope' than what the

Latvian American philosopher Judith Shklar calls the 'liberalism of fear'.[17] As Shklar sees it we must abandon the idea of having a positive goal that we all strive towards and instead promote a negative vision that we can all agree on avoiding. She believes that in a fragmented time we can agree that terror, cruelty and suffering should be avoided. Fear can unite people – it can restore the sense of community that seems to have been lost in the age of individualism. From Shklar's perspective, systematic fear is what makes political freedom possible. Descriptively Shklar may be right that today fear is a stronger motivating force than hope. Yet I agree more with Spinoza than with Shklar.

'To be alive is to be afraid,' writes Shklar.[18] And she is right about that, even if it is a pointed statement. Fear *is* fundamental to human life. It is hardly a coincidence that in the Bible the first feeling mentioned is fear – it is the first thing Adam feels after eating from the tree of knowledge. To be alive – or more correctly, to live a *human* life – is also to hope. Here it should be pointed out that Shklar does not deny that hope has a legitimate place in human life, but political hope must be a hope that does not overlook all the injustice, one that supports ideas of a wonderful future. Shklar's argument is above all anti-utopian. As she points out, historically utopias are not initially hopeful; they are laments about a present that falls short and cannot develop into anything better. They represent 'a timeless "ought" that never "is"'.[19] In this sense, one could say that utopian thinking is first and foremost an expression of political resignation, where realpolitik is abandoned in favour of fantasies. The problem increases when someone believes that these fantasies can become real. All of our biggest politically created disasters have originated this way.

Fear can seem unifying, but it more often seems divisive. It unites some but it also invites division within the community by pointing out sections of it as potential dangers. The fear Shklar writes about is the fear of losing what's most important to us. Fear undoubtedly has its place in our lives, alongside hope. When we fear something it is because we feel that something important is at stake. As the British philosopher F. H. Bradley points out, 'The man who has ceased to fear has ceased to care.'[20] The problem is that fear itself can undermine the very thing it wants to preserve. Fear undermines our freedom partly because it encourages measures that directly limit our room for agency and partly because it undermines our basic security, our sense of being able to act spontaneously in daily life without having to think about our actions in the smallest detail. As the American philosopher Michael Walzer puts it, 'the liberalism of fear presupposes the liberalism of hope, the reason being that what we are fearing for is everything we value positively.'[21]

For a liberal democracy to function, its citizens must be able to hope that they can influence society to move in a direction they find desirable. This is only viable if the citizens believe that being involved is any use, even if they don't always get what they want – and sometimes wish they hadn't got what they wanted because the consequences were nothing like what they had foreseen. Without hope there is only political apathy. In hopelessness you are paralysed, totally cut off from significant possibilities. Every hope that fades will leave you with a horizon of fewer significant possibilities, and if hope fades completely, that horizon is closed. Hope can be seen as an expression of freedom because we are not entirely at the mercy of our circumstances, but can always transcend the situation we are in.

Hope and Trust

In democratic societies we depend on each other in order to achieve political goals. We need trust. Trust requires hope. It might be even more accurate to say that trust is a form of hope. Hope is the more extensive phenomenon because you can have hope without having trust, but you cannot have trust without hope. For hope to take the form of trust you must – implicitly or explicitly – assume that it is most likely that the person or thing you are placing your trust in will prove worthy of the trust. If I were to have a guarantee that enabled me say with certainty that you would honour an agreement, for example, because the consequences of not doing so would be so disastrous to you that breaking it is inconceivable, I would have no hope or trust because they both presuppose uncertainty. If I think it is most likely that you will honour the agreement, but am not certain, I have trust in you. I may also think that it is less likely that you will honour the agreement, in which case it cannot be said that I trust you will do it, but I can still hope that you will.

Trust can thus be described as a form of hope, but it is a form of hope distinguished by us not only considering it possible that our fellow humans will act as we expect but believing that they will do so. Nevertheless, trust comes about within the framework of hope because you know there is no certainty of your fellow human acting as you expect. Trust is always associated with a risk. Here we should distinguish between blind and reflected trust. Blind trust is characterized by the fact that, despite knowing better, one ignores the risk of disappointment; one trusts something or someone unconditionally without considering that there may also be reasons to not show trust. An example of this trust is the entirely uncritical relationship cult members tend to have with their leaders. Another example could be the limitless trust some political figures have in their followers. For ardent Putinists and Trumpists there is simply nothing their political role models can say or do, no matter how crazy it may appear to outsiders, that will shake their trust. It is a form of trust that leads to fact resistance because it is not susceptible to any counterarguments. This form of trust is also defined by a complete mistrust of anything that deviates from the glossy image of one's great ideal. Why this form of trust is not desirable is obvious: in reality, it means being unenlightened and immature. As Immanuel Kant wrote in his famous essay 'What Is Enlightenment?': '*Immaturity* is the inability to use one's understanding without guidance from another.'[22] Anyone who actually uses their common sense can hardly claim that Vladimir Putin is a man to be trusted. And Donald Trump has lied so much that his words have no value.

The trust that should be cultivated in a liberal democracy is reflected trust: it is always related to an awareness of risk and always contains a grain of mistrust. Reflected trust takes our worries into account. It recognizes that there may be compelling and specific reasons for not showing trust. Reflected trust is always limited and conditional. It is hopeful rather than certain. Reflected trust is only possible when the person showing trust is willing to accept that it exposes them to a degree of risk or vulnerability. When we show trust, we specifically hope that this exposure or vulnerability is not exploited.

Trusting others means feeling confident in them and perceiving them as reliable. A well-functioning society requires its citizens to essentially view each other accordingly and to consider themselves morally obliged to appear worthy of this trust. A society can function somewhat, albeit not well, with minimal trust – as totalitarian regimes have shown – but a democratic society cannot function without trust, without citizens being confident that their basic rights and freedoms will be protected. Without such trust the democracy is built on shaky ground. On the other hand it is important to stress that a measure of distrust is crucial for democracy, not least in that citizens shouldn't just blindly trust the political leadership but rather be able to subject them to scrutiny. One might say that you have to create room for democratic mistrust in order to create democratic trust. Democratic leaders ask for reflected trust; authoritarian leaders demand blind trust.

The Hope of a Realistic Utopia

If hope is to be for a political utopia it should be limited to what the American philosopher John Rawls calls a 'realistic utopia'. It has little in common with the classical political utopias because it remains strongly connected to the world as it actually is; in fact, it should perhaps be called an ideal that we can reach for, step by step, rather a genuine utopia. A realistic utopia goes beyond mere realism in that it gives us something to strive for. It is limited to the possibility of a 'reasonable' just society, where we can reach an agreement on how this justness should be understood.[23] It presupposes that there is a reasonable pluralism in every liberal society because there is no reason to believe that rational and honest people will always come to the same conclusion after a totally free discussion.[24] We don't have to agree on why we want to reach a given goal, but we can agree on the goal itself. The point is that our tendency to idealize has to be kept in check. Our political hopes must also accept people as they are, rather than presuppose a complete transformation of human nature.[25]

A relevant political theory must deal with the possible. A realistic utopia shows us alternatives to the world we inhabit, but they are alternatives we at least have a genuine possibility of realizing. The realistic utopia brings us out of a mere longing for something better and into a reasonable hope.[26] Neither the utopian idealist nor the cynical realist has a reasonable hope: the utopian encourages us to hope for something impossible, and the cynic encourages us to abandon all hope. A realistic utopia is not to be understood as a compromise between realism and utopianism.[27] The realistic utopia is worth realizing and must be realized with morally acceptable means. The realistic utopia is not only something we can hope for but something we have reasonable grounds to hope for.

Liberal democracy must hope moderately for the realistically possible. It must not foster hopes that are beyond what it can fulfil. We cannot have a realistic utopia where all social inequality is eliminated for the simple reason that it is fundamentally impossible.[28] Nor can we have a realistic utopia where citizens don't have freedom of expression, since this would involve morally unacceptable coercion. The limits of the realistic utopia are thus partly set by what is possible and partly by what is morally acceptable. It also sets the limits for good political hope. According to Rawls we can have a reasonable hope of one day making a realistic utopia happen, which means we can also act in a way that contributes to promoting this goal.[29] A realistic utopia must be achievable under favourable conditions, but it may well be hard to accomplish. And it is necessary to state our goals and to strengthen our political hopes.

This is the liberalism of hope. Such liberalism must be open to constant revision of its goals, and not least strive for gradual improvement rather than revolutionary upheaval. It must unfold as 'piecemeal social engineering', to quote the Austrian philosopher Karl Popper, rather than as utopian engineering.[30] Instead of having to realize a definite end goal we should strive for more immediate goals – which can be demanding, of course, but not impossible to reach. Every such goal we manage to achieve will fuel the hope of realizing a better world step by step. In the American pragmatist John Dewey's democratic experimentalism, hope consists of citizens believing strongly that they can solve problems collectively, step by step. Democratic hope is a hope that democratic processes can lead us towards a better world. It is a genuine hope: it offers no guarantees. The content of this hope is left open because it depends on what problems might be pressing at any given time. Dewey also points out that we often don't understand what the problem is until we have found the solution.[31] It is a process. A process where there will be conflicts between particular interests, and the best way to handle these conflicts is by bringing them out into the open where they 'can be discussed and judged in the light of more inclusive interests than are represented by either of them separately'.[32] It is legitimate for me to pursue my own interests, my personal hopes, but the way I do it might conflict with other people's attempts to do the same. Democracy as public debate is the best way to handle such conflicts. We have to recognize that any action can lead us astray, even when we act collectively, and yet hope that we can move forward without having any solution at hand as to where we are going and how we should get there.

As the world situation currently looks, there is undoubtedly reason for discouragement. Towards the turn of the millennium all the pointers seemed to be aimed equally at the sky. There is definitely less reason for optimism now than there was just a few decades ago, but that is precisely why there is all the more room for hope. Not because our hopes should now have a higher likelihood of being fulfilled, but because hope contains resources to help us deal with the setbacks we are now experiencing. It gives us goals to reach for, goals that it will also contribute to helping us achieve.

SIX

To Hope Well and to Hope Badly

As we have seen, hope cannot generally be described as rational or irrational. A hope can be rational or irrational depending on the understanding the person hoping has of their situation and the likelihood that things will go well. It will also depend on what you hope for. We make critical assessments of our own and others' hopes. Someone who clings to hope despite the odds might be praised for being courageous or steadfast, but they might also be criticized for being foolish or unreasonable. Others, who do not hope, might be criticized for being passive or cowardly for not hoping in a situation where they should not only hope but act in accordance with that hope. They can, for example, be criticized for overestimating the likelihood of a bad outcome. We can also critically evaluate *what* we hope for. Hope contains a desire, and this desire can be aimed at good or bad objects. Both the what and how of hope can be either good or bad.

Aristotle: Hope as a Waking Man's Dream

What is perhaps the most famous Aristotelian remark about hope doesn't actually come from Aristotle's own writings, but from those of the ancient historian of philosophy Diogenes Laertius on the lives and opinions of philosophers: 'A waking man's dream'.[1] The quote corresponds well with what Aristotle writes elsewhere. Aristotle writes that dreams belong to the faculty of the senses, although as mental images they are not sensations, as such.[2] He discusses the widespread belief of his time that dreams are prophetic, which he is obviously sceptical of, claiming that it will be mostly pure coincidence if a dream turns out to correspond with a later event.[3] How then should we understand the remark that hope is like dreaming when one is awake? Hope is not prophetic. Hoping that something will happen does not mean that it will actually happen. Hope is linked to an object or event that is unavailable to the senses: something that is not, but can turn out to be. Hope is closer to imagination than sensation – it is about the possible, not the real. As mentioned, the ancient Greek 'hope' is always directed towards the future. Aristotle points out that one cannot remember the future, only the past.[4] However, one can have expectations or hopes for the future. The difference between expectation (*prosdokia*) and hope (*elpis*) apparently consists of the degree of probability that the future will bring something.

Just as happiness isn't a feeling for Aristotle – but instead consists of functioning well as a human being, which in turn creates a good feeling – hope doesn't seem to be a feeling either but rather something that creates a feeling: 'All the things that delight us when they are present also do so, for the most part, when we merely remember or expect them.'[5] Memory is not a pleasure, but thinking about something you experienced in the past can arouse pleasure. Similarly, hope is not a feeling, but it is accompanied by a feeling. To hope is to imagine a future while knowing that there is no certainty of it happening. Moreover, this future is neither impossible nor certain – hope is linked to the possible. For example, you cannot hope for immortality, even though you can always wish for it.[6]

Aristotle fully recognizes that how our lives play out is not entirely up to us, and that there is good luck and bad luck.[7] By extension he has an account of hope, and not least about 'hoping well'. Since functioning well as a human is, in one sense or another, something Aristotle likes to refer to as either a moral virtue or an intellectual virtue, we could assume that he also considers hope, at least the good hope, to be a virtue. However, hope is not mentioned among the virtues listed in Chapter Four of *Nicomachean Ethics*. He links hope to other virtues and vices, such as courage and cowardice, but does not consider it a virtue as such. Nor is hope mentioned among the emotions. And yet it is related to both virtues and emotions. It is similar to a virtue in that it is connected to one's understanding of what action is appropriate in a given situation, and it is also clear that hope, while not being a feeling in itself, is connected to one's feelings.[8]

For Aristotle one can hope in good and bad ways, and he writes about having 'reasonable hope'.[9] Young people are hopeful in a bad way because they lack experience. They have not yet experienced enough of the disappointments that life offers, and this makes them disproportionately optimistic.[10] Aristotle compares the young to drunken people since they share equally poor judgement and are easy to deceive precisely because they so quickly turn to hope. The elderly, however, are overly cautious: they have been disappointed many times and live a self-absorbed life of reminiscence instead of hope.[11] Neither group represent hoping well, but the big question is what Aristotle means by hoping well. He doesn't write much about that; however, he does write about those who hope badly. Interestingly, he never once mentions hope when describing the mature person, someone in their prime between youth and old age, who finds the middle ground and has a reasonable attitude to life.[12] Perhaps the idea is that the virtuous person, who has found the balance in life, does not need hope because he always relates to and can handle what life has to offer in the here and now. That's not what he writes, however – we just need to settle firmly that hope isn't mentioned in his account of the mature person – but he does mention hope elsewhere when describing people who function well.

Aristotle makes a distinction between the brave and the hopeful, saying that although they might behave similarly, the brave are brave because they are experienced in mastering dangerous situations, while the hopeful throw themselves into things out of excessive faith in their own abilities and the favourability of their circumstances.[13] Elsewhere, he emphasizes that the hopeful will typically be brave: 'The coward, then, is a despairing sort of person; for he fears everything. The brave man, on the other hand, has the opposite disposition; for confidence is the mark of a hopeful disposition.'[14] Aristotle seems to contradict himself here, but we can remove this contradiction by pointing out that for Aristotle the brave are those who, based on experience, take reasonable risks as opposed to the cowardly, who avoid all risks, and the foolhardy, who take irrational risks. The brave are brave because they have reason to be brave. Correspondingly, the courageous will then have such experience and insight that their hope is a good hope, while the cowardly are without hope and the reckless hope badly. Aristotle highlights sailors who, even in difficult situations, hope well 'because of their experience'.[15] It seems that for a hope to be good it must be linked to experience. A good hope must be a well-founded hope. However, Aristotle does not write much about what it means to hope in a good way except that it must be based on experience and practical reason.

What Separates Good Hope from Bad?

Like Aristotle some recent theorists distinguish between good and bad hope, but the Canadian philosopher Victoria McGeer takes things a step further by distinguishing between different *forms* of bad hope: wishful and wilful.[16] The person with wishful hope is passive and waits for other people – or other external circumstances – to realize that hope, and as a rule the person lacks a real understanding of what's required for that to happen. The person who has wilful hope, however, is active: they develop an understanding of what's required but become so one-sidedly orientated towards realizing this hope that they become reckless. As an alternative, McGeer proposes what she calls 'responsive hope'. Those with responsive hope take responsibility for what they themselves can provide but hope collectively with other people and take these other people into account. While wishful hope makes you totally dependent on other people, wilful hope makes you totally independent, and so responsive hope must find a balance between the two.

I'm not convinced by McGeer's theory, partly because it seems obvious that one can hope well alone without being part of a hopeful community and without being ruthless. But it also seems obvious that a community can hope badly if the hope is based on erroneous beliefs about likelihood or if they are hoping for the wrong thing. The hopes of mass political movements can be morally terrible and lead to ruthless actions.

Hope can be bad in many different respects: (1) an inadequate understanding of the probability of it being realized, (2) it has a bad object, (3) it requires unacceptable means for it to be realized or (4) it makes one passive instead of contributing to an improvement. A hope can also be bad in several of these respects simultaneously.

(1) A good hope depends on you having a fairly realistic understanding of the situation you – or someone you are hoping on behalf of – are in. Without this foundation a hope will be irrational. One problem here is that hope itself will easily lead us to overestimate the likelihood of a good outcome because it puts wind in the sails of our confirmation bias. With hope our attention is directed towards the desired outcome, which leads to a tendency to place emphasis on anything that points to such an outcome and to disregard

anything that indicates a bad one. Hope, therefore, contains a risk of self-deception. Just as courage can degenerate into recklessness, hope can degenerate into fancy or wishful thinking when you do not sufficiently consider the real limitations that the world places on your wishes.[17] A person that hopes well will have a realistic understanding of what might lead to their goal and what definitely won't, and of the limitations of their own agency. I can overestimate how much my actions can affect the final outcome, but I can also underestimate what is required of me and rely too much on external factors going my way. Hoping well means more than envisioning a desired outcome, it also means envisioning realistic paths to the goal along with strategies and actions that will move us forward on these paths. A good hope is also flexible. If we realize that what we are hoping for is unattainable we should change the object of our hope to something that is possible. In chaotic situations, during war or natural disasters, for example, it will often be very unclear what to hope for and how much hope is warranted, but it will be the hope available at that moment. One can hardly blame someone for hoping on shaky foundations when there are no foundations less shaky. Strictly speaking, all human actions take place on shaky foundations, but some foundations are more shaky than others.

(2) Your hope should be directed towards something worth hoping for. Hope is not value-neutral. Its value can be solely for me because what I'm hoping for will only satisfy me, or it might be good for others, ultimately all humanity and other parts of the animal kingdom or the planet. Most of our hopes are small and trivial. I'll hope that I make the next subway train and that it doesn't start raining before I get indoors. Sometimes our hopes are linked to what's most important to us, to things that will shape the rest of our lives whether they go one way or the other. Hope will often be specific, when you want something very specific to happen, but it can also be more general, such as a thought that, on the

whole, things will go well for you and your loved ones, or for that matter all humanity. Often, hope will be linked to the fact that you can achieve something better than what you have. But you can also hope for the status quo to be maintained – that the person you love will carry on loving you as long as you live or that a condition won't deteriorate as much as there might be reason to fear, that you will remain healthy well into old age, for example, despite knowing that you can't be as healthy as you were in your youth. Hope can be misplaced, however, such that I hope for something I shouldn't hope for. It can also be out of proportion to its object, such that I either hope too little or too much given the importance of what I'm hoping for. That a hope, when realized, will satisfy me or someone else is not enough for it to be considered a good hope overall if the satisfaction is contingent on another person's suffering, for example. Or suppose I had a burning hatred of an ethnic group and hoped for all the members of that group to be wiped off the face of the earth in one go. This would be a bad – or rather, downright evil – hope. A Nazi's dream of millennialism is an evil hope. The question is not only what I *can* hope for but what I *should* hope for. I must clarify for myself what I actually care about, and then I must try to clarify whether what I actually care about is what I should care about.

(3) Your hope may be directed towards an object that in isolation is perfectly fine but can only be reached via unacceptable means. For example, if I hope to seize power in a country, it is basically a legitimate hope, but if this seizure of power requires me to sabotage the democratic process, persecute opponents and so on, then it is a hope I should give up on, at least until I am aware of a situation where my goal can be reached via democratically legitimate means. It is legitimate to want wealth but not if I also believe that my hope can only be realized by committing fraud against other people. It is legitimate to hope that climate change can be

stopped, or at least limited, but this hope becomes a bad hope if you also believe that the fight against climate change can only be successful by using violent means.

(4) Hope can cause passivity by making you focus so clearly on the future that you overlook the present and so fail to see what can and should be done right now to improve the situation for you or others. Hope can also seem conserving when, by hoping, one remains in a situation that should be transcended, like a woman who stays in a relationship with a violent man based on the hope that he might change for the better, as he has promised time and time again, instead of realizing that she must leave him. In her much-quoted speech given in Davos about the climate crisis in 2019, the Swedish activist Greta Thunberg said: 'I don't want you to be hopeful. I want you to panic. I want you to feel the fear I feel every day. And then I want you to act. I want you to act as you would in a crisis. I want you to act as if the house was on fire – because it is.' In this quote Thunberg sets up a false opposition between hope and action, as though hope inevitably leads to passiveness. As I have repeatedly stressed, hope will more typically lead to action. Of course, one can also be motivated by fear instead of hope, but it is anything but obvious that fear is better suited to promoting the goal. Hope *can* make you passive, but fear can also cause total paralysis. Hope can take attention from what should be done here and now in favour of a distant goal. To follow Thunberg's rhetoric: if the house is on fire, your hope of one day successfully developing a new type of fire extinguisher is worthless. Not least in politics, losing sight of the present in favour of an imagined future can be damaging. But it is only an imagined future, a hope, that can give politics a direction.

Hope can be epistemically (1 and 4) or morally (2 and 3) faulty. Bad hope can also have its purpose, like when someone has a highly mistaken idea about the chances of avoiding a disastrous outcome, and this hope makes the situation easier for them to bear. But it's like driving a car while drunk. To hope well you must be open to what's worth hoping for and have a realistic idea of whether it can be achieved, and how.

The most efficient correction of one's hopes can be accomplished by doing one's utmost to realize them. When I was young I hoped to become a good tennis player, but what thousands of hours of practice and numerous tournaments over many years showed me was that at best I could become a decent player who could always get through a round or two – on rare occasions three – in a tournament but would never win a tournament. The fact was that I lacked natural talent, and there are limits to how much hard training can make up for such a lack. I quit at the age of seventeen because I understood that I had reached the highest level I could, which was well below the level of the best players in Norway. My hope of becoming a good tennis player was put aside, and in its place came other hopes. Hope is accompanied – at least when we hope for something of great importance to us – by reflection. This reflection can change the hope. I might realize that what I'm hoping for is not reasonably proportional to the sacrifices that need to be made in order to achieve it. Or perhaps, on the contrary, I might realize that what I was hoping for is far more important than I had envisaged and that I should put even more effort into achieving it.

A good hope has to be flexible. If your biggest worry is climate change, you might despair that the permafrost and Greenland ice sheet is melting, that our planet is losing significant amounts of both flora and fauna, that extreme weather is causing so much devastation, that the conditions for food production are deteriorating and that the widespread migration of climate refugees will cause political instability. You might despair that your hope for the so-called one-and-a-half-degree climate target cannot possibly be fulfilled. The question is how you deal with it. You might think that all hope is lost and that we may as well give up, or you might think that we may be able to manage a two-degree target. Without hope we won't even reach a three-degree target, but, with hope, we might be able to manage two. If there are no longer any realistic grounds to believe that reaching the one-and-a-half-degree target for global warming is possible, we must reorientate our hope to something that actually can be achieved. You may feel sad or angry that the one-and-a-half-degree target was missed, but anger and sorrow do not create a better world unless they are channelled towards realizing something achievable.

Such hope obliges, and it motivates us to make sacrifices now for the sake of future benefits. If you really hope, it will create a framework for your actions, for what you feel you should or must do and what you should not do. To hope well, however, you must also have an understanding of what, if anything, you *can* do: of what is possible.

SEVEN

Eternal and Finite Hope

I have a naturalistic or secular perspective on hope. Were someone to require a philosophical credo from me, I would categorize myself as a 'naturalist' in the broadest sense of the word. I assume that nothing exists beyond the natural universe, but if such a thing were to exist, then it has no influence on the natural universe and thus cannot be used to explain it. However, I do not adhere to scientism, so I do not believe that the sciences in general, or the natural sciences in particular, can tell us all that is worth knowing about human life. Besides, such naturalism would mean that we are left to ourselves with no possibility of any divine assistance, which means that thinkers who link the issue of hope very closely to a faith in God are not important to me in my investigation of hope. This is why, for example, St Augustin, St Thomas Aquinas, Søren Kierkegaard and Gabriel Marcel will not be covered to the extent some would like. Even though Aquinas, for example, has a comprehensive – and interesting – account of hope, he falls outside the scope of this investigation because all hope for him is ultimately a hope in God, since all hope is a hope for something good and God is the source of all good. For Marcel the form of hope that has genuine value is inseparable from religious faith: hope is something that must ultimately be fulfilled by God. Immanuel Kant ends up in a grey area because although he thematizes hope in a way that points towards faith in God, he remains within the realm of worldly life since faith is more grounded in hope than vice versa.

Hope for the Afterlife

It is obvious that many of those interested in hope link this hope to the afterlife. Perhaps the bulk of what's been written about hope throughout the history of philosophy is related to the afterlife as well. Is it not then a serious oversight to leave this out? Personally, I cannot see the real possibility of there being an afterlife or similar. The reason for this is that I lack understanding of what such an afterlife would be; I cannot see the real possibility of it despite being unable to rule out the logical possibility. As such I would argue that notions of an afterlife – or assistance from a supernatural power in this life – should be considered wishes rather than hopes. My mother could hope to meet my father again after they both passed away because this – according to her beliefs – was a real possibility. Personally I can at the most only imagine myself *wishing* for the same thing since it isn't a real possibility according to my own beliefs.

For the Catholic theologian and philosopher Augustine, it is clear that the only real hope is the hope that is linked to God:

As, therefore, we are saved, so we are made happy by hope. And as we do not as yet possess a present, but look for a future salvation, so is it with our happiness, and this 'with patience'; for we are encompassed with evils, which we ought patiently to endure, until we come to the ineffable enjoyment of unmixed good; for there shall be no longer anything to endure. Salvation, such as it shall be in the world to come, shall itself be our final happiness. And this happiness these philosophers refuse to believe in, because they

do not see it, and attempt to fabricate for themselves
a happiness in this life, based upon a virtue which is
as deceitful as it is proud.[1]

I am obviously cast in the same mould as 'these philosophers'
Augustine refers to. One could object that even if eternal bliss
were to be the grand prize it is hardly futile to hope for any
consolation prize that might be on a slightly lower shelf. If you
cannot be satisfied with what's genuinely possible, but also
have a need for the impossible to get through life, a secular
hope will not be enough. If all hope is linked to the afterlife,
there is no room for hope for the worldly life.

A problem with religious hope is that it can displace the
secular hope – for example, the 'knight of faith' by the Danish
existentialist philosopher Søren Kierkegaard. This figure has
undergone a double movement: at first, through 'infinite
resignation' he has given up all hope connected to this world,
but then he regains all that he has lost, through faith. He who
is infinitely resigned turns away from the worldly and instead
makes eternal bliss his goal. It is not something that is done
once and for all. You will be constantly tempted to attach
your hope to the temporal world and your resignation must
therefore be performed repeatedly. We could say the infinite
resignation makes faith almost unavoidable. What characterizes this knight of faith is that even after something he has
apparently hoped for is fulfilled, he can state that he remains
'exactly the same'.[2] The knight of faith may also have his wishes
and hopes connected to his earthly life, but it really does not
matter to him whether they are fulfilled or not. No matter
what loss he suffers, he experiences himself as unchanged.
One could alternately say that the knight of faith has cut
himself off from any experience of loss. Kierkegaard writes
that the believer possesses the only sure antidote to despair
since everything is possible with God.[3] For such a believer
nothing is impossible, nothing is irreparable and no loss is

definitive. But to cut yourself off from the experience of loss is to cut yourself off from the experience that something in this life can really mean something. The knight of faith appears to participate in the world but only vaguely. If such a knight of faith pretends to be someone's close friend, for example, but can simply state that he is the same following said friend's death, he was never a true friend. If you care about someone and they die, it changes you – you will never be the same again because you are marked by the loss.

The knight of faith lives only seemingly among people in the temporal world: he is 'incognito', as Kierkegaard puts it, because his real life is not here on earth.[4] Kierkegaard then goes on to describe this figure, how if he is offered everything this world has to offer he might accept it while shrugging his shoulders a little, and if the world takes everything from him he will also shrug his shoulders. Nothing in this world, not even other people, can really mean anything to him. For example, if you love another person, you can be rejected. You will be at the mercy of something external, something you cannot control. The knight of faith, on the other hand, does not have to deal with anything external beyond his own faith. The knight of faith has made himself invulnerable. Admittedly Kierkegaard claims that the knight of faith finds joy in his worldly life, in his work and relationships with others, but it should be described as a hollow joy since nothing is ever really at stake. The knight of faith is unconcerned and can suffer no loss because all his hopes are attached to God, not temporal things. The knight of faith is a good Christian, because as Jesus says in the Gospel of Matthew (10:37): 'Whoever loves father or mother more than me is not worthy of me; and whoever loves son or daughter more than me is not worthy of me.' The price the knight of faith pays is that nothing he surrounds himself with can really matter. It is an impoverished life. If the price of hoping for eternity is having to write off all real hope for this life, the price is too high.[5]

Impermanence as a Requirement for Meaning in Life

The pain of living, of invariably having to experience the loss of something irreplaceable, is not in itself attractive. Without this pain, however, you cannot live a life *worth* living, if by 'worth living' you mean a life that contains meaning and genuine joy. But the pain of living is unavoidable for the vast majority of people, as Augustine also experienced. He reproached himself for crying when his mother died, as it meant he was attaching himself far too strongly to the worldly, the transient, when the only thing that matters is beyond this world.[6] Some time later, however, he claimed: 'my heart has been healed of that wound, in which I could be blamed for a too-worldly affection.'[7] If so, I'd say the cure was worse than the disease.

The relationship with those you love – indeed, with everything you care about – vanishes in eternity. Everything that would normally mean something to you in life as you know it becomes more or less irrelevant. For Augustine all love of finite things, and that would also apply to all hope for finite things, must be rejected because it makes us vulnerable. It makes what we love or hope for something we can lose. But where the Stoic solution to this problem was to attempt to eliminate the emotions from life in order to gain complete rational mastery of oneself, Augustine did not believe that this was possible, arguing that you must still love but you must direct your love towards God rather than the worldly:

> God of hosts, turn us and show your face, and we shall be saved. For wherever the human soul turns, it is fixed upon sorrows unless it turns to you – even if it is fixed upon beautiful things outside you and outside itself, beautiful things that would be nothing at all if they were not from you.[8]

You will only escape sorrow by looking away from the earthly and towards God. You will lose nothing in eternity.[9] It's natural to think that you can't lose anything if nothing happens.

Our lives are filled with projects, activities that unfold over time, some of them more important to us than others. They might involve getting an education, working, training to be good at a sport or practising a musical instrument, writing a book, maintaining and nurturing friendships and family relationships. Some of these projects will be closer to our core identity than others, but which of them is most central will vary from person to person. When the most important projects fall apart, it feels like you have lost a vital part of yourself. These projects, which are expressions of what we care about, give life structure and direction.

We are willing to make sacrifices in the present for the sake of these projects. Writing a paper can be terribly boring, and you might have to stay home on a Friday night and work instead of enjoying yourself at a party, in order to meet a deadline and complete your degree. Anyone who has played a sport at a competitive level knows that you sometimes have to play while injured, and that it hurts, but you accept that pain because you have a goal that extends beyond the present. In any relationship there will be hard and painful episodes and periods; it might seem easier to leave but you stay because you see the relationship as part of your future. The future affects the present because our life is structured by such projects. In the end all projects dissolve because, as the British economist John Maynard Keynes points out: 'In the long run, we are all dead.'[10] It is by no means unwise to remember that one day you will die, because death puts a frame around life. We humans are apparently the only animals that are aware that we are born and that we will die, and this gives life a unique framework.

When our projects are so important to us, it is not least because our options are so limited. For example, I have to choose my book projects carefully because I only have time to write a few of the many books I would like to write. Had time been infinite, I would have written not only all my unwritten books but *all* books. However, if I could write an infinite number of books, none of them would mean anything to me. Eternal life would be meaningless. Limitations are what make something more significant than something else. As E. M. Cioran points out: 'We can conceive of eternity only by eliminating all the perishable, all that counts for us.'[11]

The time I spend with those I care about most is valuable because it is limited. An infinite amount of time is valueless time. We cannot separate ourselves from the fact that the value of time is contingent on its scarcity – that time becomes more valuable the scarcer it is. And yet, if I live to be one hundred, a single day will be no less valuable than if I live to be seventy. If I have a relationship with someone that spans many decades, every hour we spend together will be no less valuable than the time I spend with someone I'm in a relationship with for one week – on the contrary, because meaningful relationships take time to build. There is no given amount of meaning that has to be distributed over the time at one's disposal, but time must have an end for meaning to occur. My death is not in itself meaningful, but it is necessary in order for my life to be so.

We can also illustrate this using the relationships we have with our pets. Had the pets I have owned in my life not been vulnerable, had they not needed food and care or been able to get sick and die, I would have had an entirely different relationship with them. I wouldn't have cared about them as much as I did. I wouldn't have *cared for* an invulnerable dog. When a puppy comes into your life, you know that it will most likely die long before you. Since I have had pets my entire life, dogs and cats, I have also experienced them getting sick, injured and dying. I have taken them to the vet, terrified that this is the end, and waited hopefully for word that their treatment has gone well. So far I have outlived all my pets, and the grief has been considerable every time one has died. That grief is the price you pay for the love of this animal. It is testament to the sincerity of the relationship.

We are vulnerable and exposed, and that vulnerability is necessary in order for something to have meaning. Aristotle points out that he who does not believe that he can be hurt by anything does not fear anything either.[12] Such a person cannot hope for anything either. Such a person cannot actually care about anything, since caring about something presupposes that something is at stake. Meaning in life comes from caring about something, and those who care become vulnerable. If you love someone, you have no guarantee that the person you love will not be taken away from you in an accident or that the relationship will fall apart. That is why it is precious. A life without vulnerability is a life without meaning.

Franz Kafka put it this way in a conversation with his friend Max Brod after determining that God had a bad day when he created us: 'Plenty of hope – for God – no end of hope – only not for us.'[13] But it is of course the opposite: for God there is no hope, because for God everything is possible. Only vulnerable, finite beings like us, who do not have full control, can hope, and preferably if we do not put our trust in God.

EIGHT

What Can I Hope For?
Immanuel Kant and Maria von Herbert

In *Critique of Pure Reason* (1781) the German philosopher Immanuel Kant writes that all the interests of reason unite in the following three questions:

> What can I know?
> What ought I to do?
> What may I hope?[1]

The first question is answered by examining man's cognitive abilities, the second by examining the moral standards provided by man's own reason and the third by examining what man himself can do to be happy and deserve happiness. The first question is theoretical, the second practical and the third is both. The answers to the first two questions are what force the third: since the answers stipulate limits to what I can know and do, they create room for hope. As we will see, the third question takes Kant right up to – and perhaps beyond – the border of speculative philosophy and theology.

Kant's discussions on hope are somewhat on the periphery of what we normally understand by hope. Since Kant is known as one of philosophy's greatest optimists and actually believes that we have a moral obligation to be optimists, one might think that he believes we have good reason to live in hope. However, his descriptions of human existence are truly depressing. When he describes how a human life appears, he is only slightly more cheerful than classic pessimists like Schopenhauer, who we will consider in the next chapter. It is not without reason that Goethe, after reading Kant's lectures on anthropology, claimed that Kant portrays all life 'like some malignant disease and the world like a madhouse'.[2]

Kant received three letters from a young woman named Maria von Herbert, who was an avid reader of his works and the sister of Baron Franz Paul von Herbert, who was also a dedicated reader. The first letter came in August 1791, in which she asks him 'for help, for solace, or for counsel to prepare me for death'.[3] She says that although his philosophy proves that there is a life after death, 'I have found nothing, nothing at all that could replace the good I have lost.' She elaborates that it concerns a relationship with a man who no longer loves her after she told a lie for a long time, even though this lie didn't hide anything unfavourable about her. Had she not read Kant's ethics, where suicide is deemed morally unacceptable, she would have undoubtedly killed herself, she writes, but she finds nothing that can help her live: 'Now put yourself in my place and either damn me or give me solace.' The letter undoubtedly falls short in terms of spelling and punctuation, and this may have caused Kant to take the woman less seriously than he should, but it was not unusual for women during this period to be poor spellers because they did not receive much education. Either way, the letter testifies to an author who is able to think philosophically and on principle. Kant takes Herbert seriously enough to reply.[4] In a sense she forced him to reply since she pointed out that the categorical imperative required him to do so. However, the reply is rather underwhelming. Herbert sends Kant an existential cry of anguish, and she gets a brief and didactic explanation about truth and lies in return followed by a claim that the man's love will gradually return if she demonstrates that she has improved her character. If that didn't happen the man's affection was probably 'more physical than moral' and would have disappeared eventually anyway, and this is simply one of the blows life deals us that we have to deal with. He adds: 'since the value of life, insofar as it consists of the enjoyment we can get out of people, is generally overestimated.' What's striking about Kant's reply is that it responds so little to her problem: she writes that her heart is broken, that she sees no point in living and that nothing in Kant's philosophy has helped her in the slightest with that problem.

This young woman did not vanish from Kant's mind and, after a long period of not hearing from her, he wrote to one of her friends, with whom he also corresponded, asking him what effect his letter had had on the woman. That in turn led to a new, more extensive letter from her, which arrived more than a year after the first. It begins with her apologizing for taking so long to reply, noting that she was satisfied with the answer she had received. She goes on to say that the warm feelings her beloved once felt for her had returned but that, although she is happy for him, she no longer sees any point in the relationship, which for her has become only a banal pleasure. She then writes:

> My vision is clear and I have the sense of constantly reproaching myself and I get an empty feeling that extends inside me and all around me, so that I am almost superfluous to myself. Nothing attracts me, and even getting every possible wish I might have would not give me any pleasure, nor is there a single thing that seems worth the trouble of doing.[5]

She refers to this as 'a boredom that makes my life unbearable', and that she has only one wish, namely 'to shorten this so useless life of mine, a life in which I am convinced I shall become neither better nor worse'.

Herbert asks Kant to investigate this question – presumably about what might make life worth living – or failing that perhaps offer something that might help her deal with 'this unbearable emptiness of soul'. While the first letter showed a woman who was upset, the next is more apathetic. There is no longer any desire: all is emptiness. It is tempting to say that Herbert anticipates the French author Albert Camus' *The Myth of Sisyphus* (1942) by 150 years, where Camus famously opens the work with the words: 'There is but one truly serious philosophical problem, and that is suicide. Judging whether life is or is not worth living amounts to answering the fundamental question of philosophy.'[6] We can, of course, point out that Camus may have got a little carried away – and Herbert too, perhaps – because people can of course kill themselves for other reasons than finding life as such not worth living, and one can, for that matter, think that life is not worth living and still not commit suicide. After all, few of the great pessimists have ended their own lives. Either way, Herbert's question presents Kant with a philosophical problem: what can make life worth living?

Kant evidently did not reply to this letter, since there are no draft replies among his papers and von Herbert's next letter in the spring of 1794 indicates that she did not receive any reply from him.[7] In this letter, she writes that she has found peace after loathing life for so long and that she realizes that although death is preferable from an individual perspective, this attraction to death can be held in check by focusing on one's friends and the demands of morality. She then thanks Kant for the attention he has given her.

In 1803, when she was 33 years old, Maria von Herbert disappeared. Her body was never found, but her brother assumed she had killed herself, defending her act as courageous rather than an expression of weakness.[8] Her brother, incidentally, committed suicide in 1811. However, the point of mentioning this story is not to blame Kant for the woman's suicide. Kant presumably answered her first letter to the best of his ability and probably didn't realize the seriousness of her second. Herbert's third letter indicated that she had somehow come through the life crisis – or perhaps that she had given up hoping that Kant could help her with it. There were also a number of other factors that contributed to making Herbert's situation difficult, without Kant knowing, such as the fact that she had given birth to a child out of wedlock. The only directly reprehensible thing Kant did was perhaps to forward Herbert's letter to the daughter of one of his friends, warning her against being led astray by her imagination as 'the ecstatical little lady' had done. The point is that Herbert puts her finger on something in Kant's philosophy: she asks for meaning, and Kant is only able to give her morality. She asks for hope in this life, and the only hope Kant can offer lies beyond this life.

Kant's answer to the question of what I can hope for is basically that I cannot hope for much in this life, but that I can hope to attain the *summum bonum*, the ultimate good, specifically a state in which I am not just happy but *deserve* happiness, in a life after this. Furthermore, I can hope that after I am gone the human race will continue to progress towards a state of moral perfection.

Kant defines hope as an affect that is aroused 'when the prospect of immeasurable good fortune opens unexpectedly'.[9] It's a peculiar definition. First, hope does not necessarily have to be about 'immeasurably good fortune' because it is normally related to something much smaller than that. Second, one can also hope for something other than good fortune. Third, it is funny to use the expression 'unexpected' given that hope needs to be linked to something one perceives as possible. Anyway, according to Kant hope is always a hope for good fortune, and it is a good fortune we are not guaranteed to achieve. He would basically go so far as to say that we are more or less guaranteed not to find happiness in this life.

We must all be free to seek happiness as we see fit, provided we do not thereby do so at the expense of other people's freedom.[10] This is connected to one of Kant's basic ideas that the unique thing about humans compared with all other animals is that humans are 'an end in themselves', meaning more specifically that humans have an ability to define their own life goals, and because of this ability they also have the right to do so. Kant rejects a state where the authorities decide how the citizens will be happy as 'the greatest despotism imaginable'. The goal for everyone will always be happiness, but happiness, as such, is indefinite. No one else can define your happiness for you. So everyone should have the right to seek happiness as he sees fit, but Kant is convinced that such a pursuit of happiness is doomed to fail. Kant believes that human life, taken as a whole, is a rather bleak phenomenon. In a footnote from *Critique of Judgement* (1790) he is very explicit:

> It is easy to decide what sort of value life has for us if it is assessed merely by what one enjoys (the natural end of the sum of all inclinations, happiness). Less than zero: for who would start life anew under the same conditions, or even according to a new and self-designed plan (but one still in accord with the course of nature), which would, however, still be aimed merely at enjoyment?[11]

Kant therefore believes that it is obvious that the evils in a human life need to be greater than the good and that one must also be allowed to choose a new life plan, provided one stays within the limits set by nature. In his essay 'Conjectural Beginning of Human History', he writes that 'to be sure, one must understand only partly how to assess the worth of this life if one can still wish it to last longer than it actually does; for that would only be to prolong a play which is a constant grappling with nothing but troubles.'[12] In other words, human life as such, as it plays out within our limited time on earth, is incompatible with happiness. This doesn't necessarily mean we cannot have moments of happiness in between all the misery but rather that the total will inevitably be negative.

When Kant offers Maria von Herbert so few comforting words about what happiness she can achieve in her earthly life, it is presumably because he believes there isn't that much to say and considers serving her with comforting untruths totally unacceptable. When he offers her nothing but ethics, after her asking him for the meaning of life, it is because he believes that to measure the value of life based on the happiness we might attain is to use the wrong yardstick. Our value as human beings does not lie most fundamentally in our ability to experience happiness, but in our ability to act morally. Kant's discussions of hope in *Critique of Pure Reason* (1781) and *Critique of Practical Reason* (1788) relate to the prospect of being happy – more specifically to the prospect of being happy because I have acted morally well. Our reason demands this to be possible.[13] We can see that it is not inevitable that the morally good person does well, in that they become happy, or that the morally bad person does badly. We must therefore assume that we have an immortal soul and that some being exists that keeps track of everything, namely God, so that the realization of the *summum bonum*, which is the union of virtue and happiness, can be realized after we have left our worldly existence behind.[14]

According to Kant, anyone who truly scrutinizes themselves – and he believes that we all have a duty to do this – will find that they fall short as a human being and will always fall short in our earthly life. One can therefore hope to be able to continue improving oneself, in a life after this, to at least have an imagined opportunity to reach the goal. Our own reason demands we do everything in our power and then hope that anything not in our power may turn out well for us, even if we don't possess knowledge of any higher power that can help us. Such a higher power is a necessary prerequisite if our desire for happiness is to become a hope for happiness because simply making ourselves happy is beyond our control.[15]

As Kant sees it religion has almost no other function besides supporting morality. From the perspective of reason, a literal understanding of the Bible can be considered no more than superstition. Here Kant takes a more radical position in the last part of his authorship than he did previously, when, as he formulated it, he had established a limit to our knowledge in order to create room for our faith. Kant's God is not some form of person, whom you have a relationship to, but an idea of reason, shaped by reason in its attempt to achieve rational self-determination. Someone who prays is really just talking to themselves, to their own reason, not to an independently existing figure with whom one can have a relationship.

In Kant's writings on the philosophy of history, he has another – and in my opinion more interesting, although not necessarily more convincing – approach to hope. According to Kant we are morally obliged to be optimists. He makes no clear distinction between optimism and hope, and we might perhaps say that optimism takes hope's place. He claims that we should realize our human nature as much as possible, and this can only happen by reshaping the world so that it complies with our reason. Since we are a moral species, we must create reasonable cultures that are consistent with our rational nature. So far our task seems to be progress. However, Kant claims that progress is furthered not just by us trying to act well, but by nature forcing it to happen.[16] It is precisely because we are vulnerable beings, surrounded by inhospitable nature and living together despite also seeking power over each other, that humanity can move forward. Every agony or misfortune can be explained by the fact that, in the end, it will all be for the better. All the pain we feel is there to make us better people.[17] All the evil we do to each other can be explained as being part of a whole that is progressing towards the realization of good. Kant stresses that his theory of progress cannot be proven but that it is useful for giving our actions a sense of purpose in a larger perspective.[18] What is central to Kant's idea of progress is not the individual but the human race. You cannot hope for much in your own life, but you can hope for humankind. Kant believes that we are obliged to believe in progress because faith itself will promote progress towards a better world.

Our reason cannot oversee all causal relationships, so we cannot say with any certainty how humanity will ultimately fare, and this in itself creates room for hope.[19] Kant claims that we are morally obliged to hope because hope is a necessary requirement for our moral motivation.[20] Without hope we would resign instead of act as morality requires us to act. Is this a rational basis for hope? Kant thinks so – at least, that it isn't irrational. As long as the object of a hope is not impossible, it isn't irrational to hope.

There are thus two types of hope in Kant's philosophy. The first is aimed at our individual lives; it is about being able to achieve the highest good, the combination of happiness and virtue. The second is aimed at the human race and involves the completion of our species through the creation of a world in which everyone acts well and history has thereby reached its goal. Neither of them appears to be especially satisfactory. What Kant offers in *Critique of Pure Reason* and *Critique of Practical Reason* is a description of specific hope that must also be realized in the hereafter, rather than hope as a more general phenomenon of human life. In the writings on the philosophy of history, he seems to be advocating optimism more than hope. Although Kant proclaims that one of philosophy's three main questions is the question of what I can hope for, he basically gives no account of the ordinary, secular hope that can be realized within the framework of a human life. From what he does say about such hope it is tempting to summarize that he considers human life to be fairly hopeless.

When Kant nevertheless insists so strongly on the necessity of hope it is because he believes that we would otherwise be crushed by desperation or just settle for wishing for a better life after this one. Either of these will prevent us from striving, as we should, to make *this* world better. Without hope we will fall short as moral agents. And I believe Kant is right about that, but I don't see that we necessarily have to hope in exactly the way Kant describes. A lesser hope than one for the ultimate good and a world of people who are all moral paragons might be enough.

Is Kant's hope sufficient? It wasn't for Maria von Herbert, and it probably isn't for a great many of us. The hope Kant offers seems exceedingly tenuous. Or perhaps, more specifically, too remote: the objects of his hope lie beyond this life. I won't deny that a highly relevant hope can extend beyond one's own lifetime, such as when the Russian poet Anna Akhmatova found meaning in life by hoping that the elegy she wrote between 1935 and 1961, 'Requiem' (1963), would be a testimony about Stalin's terror for generations to come. It is nevertheless a closer, less abstract hope than hoping that humanity will at some point in the future reach a state of moral perfection, and that you are a part of this process.

The German philosopher Theodor W. Adorno argues that Kant's critical philosophy is an effort to save dogmatic metaphysics in a non-dogmatic way.[21] Where dogmatic thinkers claimed to have knowledge that goes beyond what we can experience – about God and the immortality of the soul – Kant draws us back within the limits of experience. At the same time Kant claims that if life is to make sense to us we must imagine that God exists and that there is an existence after this life. According to Adorno, Kant realizes how unbearable the existing world is but attempts to mobilize a hope, against all reason, since despair is 'unthinkable'. At the same time, Adorno agrees with Kant: 'Without hope there is no good.'[22] Adorno's main objection to Kant is not that Kant hopes but that his hope has a false positivity that is a form of wishful thinking. According to him, the world after Auschwitz shows that we have no reason for hope.[23] For Adorno the world as we experience it gives us nothing to hope for, but he nevertheless believes that we must allow room for hope in that we can neither know nor imagine what we are hoping for. This hope couldn't be any more empty. The only conceivable hope for Adorno is what Jonathan Lear calls 'radical hope', which he describes as the mere possibility that something good will happen.[24] Lear's concept of radical hope will be discussed in more detail in Chapter Ten.

Kant is officially an optimist, one who even claims that we are morally obliged to be optimists, but on closer inspection he turns out to be more of a pessimist as far as individual human life is concerned. It is striking how agreed Kant the 'optimist' and Adorno the 'pessimist' are on the description of the world we inhabit as being somewhere we basically have very little to hope for; however, Kant claims that we can *think* beyond what is yielded from experience, without it being *knowledge* of something we cannot experience, while Adorno would say that we cannot even think beyond this experience, but we can keep the door open to the fact that there might be something to hope for without being able to tell what it is.

We don't necessarily have to accept Kant's and Adorno's descriptions of the world's miserable condition. Instead, we can claim that the reality we experience is precisely what gives us considerable room for hope.

NINE

Optimism, Pessimism and Hope

The Czech author, dissident and politician Václav Havel draws a distinction between hope and optimism, saying that hope is not a belief that things will go 'well' but instead that things will 'make sense', however things may turn out.[1] It is an unusual understanding of hope. He links it to things that 'clearly transcend the horizon of our own lives', but he says very little about how this transcendence should be understood.[2] I won't speculate on what Havel means more specifically, but I agree in any case that we can and should distinguish between hope and optimism. Hope is fully compatible with both optimism and pessimism, as long as one's optimism or pessimism does not degenerate into the absolute certainty that things have to go well or badly, respectively, but rather maintains that things will most likely go really well or really badly. It is easier to separate specific hope from optimism than generalized hope. For generalized hope the vague belief that things will probably go well is confusingly similar to optimism, provided the optimism does not degenerate into absolute certainty.

In everyday speech we often use the word 'optimism' as a slightly disparaging term for wishful thinking, while 'pessimism' should be the realistic and mature position. On the other hand 'pessimism' is also used disparagingly about anaemic doom-mongers, while 'optimism' is synonymous with courage and bravery. The very terms 'optimism' and 'pessimism' are modern. Both were originally coined during philosophical debates as negative labels for one's opponents. The word 'optimism' appears for the first time in 1737 in a critique of G. W. Leibniz, and 'pessimism' in a critique of Voltaire in 1759. Both 'pessimist' and 'optimist' were originally what we might call philosophical invectives, a kind of philosophical insult, similar to how words like 'neoliberalist' or 'postmodernist' are often used today. There are ways of thinking, not least pessimistically, that are much older than these expressions. It is, for example, no stretch to claim that the book of Ecclesiastes in the Old Testament is almost boundlessly pessimistic. Likewise, the philosopher Hegesias of Cyrene in Greek antiquity was called the 'death persuader' because he gave such a bleak description of human life that many of his followers committed suicide.

In an excellent study of the philosophical history of pessimism from Pierre Bayle to Arthur Schopenhauer, the Dutch philosopher Mara van der Lugt distinguishes between value-orientated and future-orientated versions of pessimism and optimism.[3] Of these, the future-orientated version is closest to how the expressions are most commonly used today. By future-orientated we mean more accurately that, strictly speaking, only an optimist expects something definite from the future, namely that it will be better than the present, while a pessimist can only content himself with saying that we cannot expect anything definite from the future – it is simply not something we can place our trust in. Value-orientated optimism and pessimism are more symmetrical: they do not concern the passage of time, but whether the world's existence is fundamentally of good or evil.[4]

From hereon in I will deal mostly with the future-orientated variant since I am interested in the question of what hope we can attach to the future. We might note that early critics of optimism, such as Voltaire, argued that it failed precisely because it was incompatible with hope. If one claims, like Leibniz, that we live in 'the best of all possible worlds', there is no room for hope, simply because the world cannot be better than it already is. It would then obviously be based on a static, value-orientated notion of optimism, which is an argument that has no relevance to future-orientated optimism. Both the optimist and the pessimist would like to claim to have morality on their side. Kant justifies his optimism, among other things, by the fact that we must be optimistic to avoid becoming morally demotivated, while Schopenhauer, for his part, claims that optimism causes us to overlook or make excuses for the world's suffering, so that only absolute pessimism can help develop the compassion he regards as being the core of morality.

Schopenhauer: The High Priest of Pessimism

If we should choose one pessimist from the history of philosophy and give them a slightly broader presentation, it is hard to avoid Schopenhauer. When I read Schopenhauer I am often reminded of the crazy artist described in the Irish writer Samuel Beckett's *Endgame* (1957):

> I once knew a madman who thought the end of the world had come. He was a painter – and engraver. I had a great fondness for him. I used to go and see him, in the asylum. I'd take him by the hand and drag him to the window. Look! There! All that rising corn! And there! Look! The sails of the herring fleet! All that loveliness!
>
> He'd snatch away his hand and go back into his corner. Appalled. All he had seen was ashes.[5]

Schopenhauer differs from the painter in not being particularly confused, but his perspective is just as bleak and he is equally impervious to anything that might lighten the picture a bit. For Schopenhauer, the world must be described as a 'hell' that should never have existed at all.[6] He dismisses the theory of optimism as 'a truly wicked way of thinking, a bitter mockery of the unspeakable sufferings of humanity'.[7] The lack of consideration lies in the optimist explaining away the suffering rather than taking it seriously. The many sufferings cannot be arranged into a whole that gives them meaning. If one really takes all the world's suffering into account, it stands in stark contrast to any imagined excellence. Where Leibniz claims that we live in the best of all possible worlds, Schopenhauer claims, on the contrary, that it can be called the worst of all possible worlds.[8] With such a bleak description of life, one could imagine that hoping for something better would seem like an attractive alternative. That is definitely not the path Schopenhauer takes.

Section 313 in Schopenhauer's *Parerga and Paralipomena* (1851) deserves to be quoted in its entirety:

> Hope is confusing the wish for an event with its probability. But perhaps no one is free from the foolishness of the heart that so strongly distorts the intellect's correct assessment of probability that it regards one in a thousand as an easily possible case. And yet a hopeless misfortune resembles a quick death blow, whereas a constantly thwarted and repeatedly revived hope resembles a slow torturous death.

> Whoever has been abandoned by hope has also been abandoned by fear; this is the meaning of the expression 'desperate'. For it is natural for a human being to believe what he desires, and to believe it because he desires it. Now when this benevolent, soothing peculiarity of his nature is wiped out by repeated, extremely harsh blows of fate and he is even brought around to the reverse situation of believing that what

he does not desire must happen while what he desires never could, simply because he desires it, then this is precisely the state which we have called despair.[9]

Schopenhauer defined humankind as a 'metaphysical animal', and metaphysics is exactly where the problem lies. Metaphysics gives us an understanding of ourselves and others, about the universe and our own mortality. All other animals simply reproduce; they don't ask why. But we require an answer. The animal is far more content with its existence than the human, precisely because it does not have the ability to hope.[10] Humans live under the yoke of time in a way that animals do not, precisely because animals live in the present. We humans are self-aware, and we can think about things that aren't there, events that have happened in the past or might happen in the future, not least the prospect of dying. Animals can suffer as well, but they cannot suffer from what is yet to be. Animals do not hope for future pleasures, which, according to Schopenhauer, will mostly turn out to be future disappointments.

It is hope that fuels our desires, and these desires are what really cause us pain. The solution must therefore be to minimize hope so that the desires vanish too and cannot cause us further suffering.[11] We cannot change who we are. We cannot become animals that are content with living in the here and now. We cannot wish for an animal's life. All that remains otherwise is to give a resounding no to life itself. As Schopenhauer sees it, the ultimate reason for not hoping is that there is nothing worth hoping for in human life which just 'swings back and forth like a pendulum between pain and boredom'.[12] Humanity's most fundamental interest is to avoid the suffering that is the essence of life, but if suffering is repressed, life becomes boring. If the person succeeds in breaking the boredom, the suffering will return.[13] There is no possible upside here, and hope is destructive because it fools us into believing that there might be other options. There is no satisfaction other than temporary freedom from suffering. Hope confuses us and makes us suffer because we think there might be something more than that. However, we can say that Schopenhauer hopes for one thing, namely that hope can be overcome. He also finds a degree of solace in art, especially in music, where for a brief moment you can lose yourself in aesthetic bliss.

What should one say to a pessimist like Schopenhauer? Perhaps only that his description of human life is incorrect according to your experience of life; that you actually find it meaningful, that you have found that not all hopes end in disappointment and so on. Stating that anyone who experiences life in a more positive light has to be living in denial, or is blinded by an illusion, isn't convincing. And if Schopenhauer's pessimism isn't very convincing, neither is his rejection of hope. Another question is whether the optimist has a more convincing position than the pessimist.

Who Is Right, the Optimist or the Pessimist?

Can we determine if the pessimist or the optimist is right in their evaluation of the world? I myself am a renegade pessimist. Until I was about thirty years old I would probably have been described as relatively pessimistic, but things have changed since then and today I would probably claim that I am moderately optimistic. Of course, I know more today than I did when I was thirty, but I still don't think we can say that my changed attitude has been caused by a greater supply of facts. It is perhaps most comparable to a change in what Wittgenstein calls 'seeing aspects'.[14] One of Wittgenstein's essential points in his theory is that we can make ourselves see a phenomenon in a different way. A change in seeing aspects implies a change in what one sees, even if one is looking at the same thing. The object appears to both change and not change. But what changes is the gaze. Optimism and pessimism lie more in the *looking* at historical facts than in the facts themselves. There are no separate courses for optimists and pessimists: they relate to the same history, but they interpret it differently and emphasize different aspects as being particularly central. Both optimism and pessimism are also quite impervious to facts. They are happy to let a reference to the whole override all the individual cases that might contradict them.

For example, the French philosopher Jean-Jacques Rousseau distinguishes between the fact that absolutely all things are good and that the whole is good, writing that the latter claim does not mean that every evil must be explained away. Rousseau continues that the question of whether this optimism is right cannot be decided by referring to events in the material world, it can only be done according to God's attributes – since God is supposed to be good, it follows that the world as a whole is good.[15] Anything that does not contribute to progress, or that even points in the opposite direction, is dismissed as irrelevant because it does not fit into a whole that is already positively defined. The optimist is aware of the world's evils but places them within a whole that is claimed nevertheless to be going in the right direction. This easily leads to the absurd explaining away of all evils, which is duly parodied in Voltaire's *Candide* (1759). After being struck by all kinds of misfortunes, Candide concludes that optimism is a 'mania for insisting that all is well when one is suffering'.[16] The pessimist believes that there is no meaningful whole that can justify individual evils, and they will claim either that the very notion of such a whole is illusory or that there is a whole that makes everything worse. Pessimism does not have to be a notion that everything will change for the worse – it can mean that the world will remain just as terrible.

Even if you were to think that the world has significantly developed for the better, it won't automatically lead to optimism. You will have only established that the world has developed in a certain way until now. An optimist is someone who claims that this positive development will continue, while a pessimist will be able to acknowledge that things have gone very well until now but also claim that things will now change. Both optimism and pessimism come in hopeful and totally certain variants. The totally certain variant thinks there is a certainty that things will go well or badly, while the hopeful variant thinks that the outcome is uncertain but might go well. Hopeful optimism and pessimism can be distinguished by the predominance of probability, by whether they believe that the outcome is more likely to be good or more likely to be bad. As pointed out earlier hope in itself does not require a pre-dominance of probability. One can think that the likelihood of a good outcome is vanishingly small but still be hopeful. That is why there are hopeful pessimists.

The optimist is not necessarily hopeful. If I am sufficiently optimistic – so optimistic that I totally rule out any possibilities other than those I would like to see realized – there is no room for hope, because hope requires uncertainty. If, in a state of uncertainty, I believe that it is overwhelmingly more likely that things will not go the way I want but that there is a possibility of a good outcome, and I attach great importance to this possibility, I am hopeful but pessimistic. A patient who accepts a prognosis that gives him a 5 per cent chance of survival cannot, by definition, be optimistic about the way the disease will progress, but he can attach considerable hope to the fact that there *is* a 5 per cent chance of survival. As I write these sentences, I still consider it most likely that Russia will prove too strong militarily for Ukraine – despite Ukraine's impressive resistance – but I sincerely hope that the Ukrainian forces will manage to offer enough resistance to make Putin finally realize that this war cannot be won and withdraw his forces. Hope and optimism often accompany each other, but not necessarily so.

The disagreement between the optimist and the pessimist cannot be resolved by referring to facts. An optimist and a pessimist can, in principle, relate to exactly the same facts and yet end up in diametrically opposed positions. Both optimism and pessimism are more of an attitude, a perspective on what the world is offering us, and therefore cannot be disproven by referring to what they are a perspective on. We can say that it is not a question of facts but of what the facts mean. Having said that, both the pessimist and the optimist would sooner refer to facts, and preferably facts that are a particularly striking expression of their perspective on the world. The problem is that this doesn't necessarily have as big an impact on the person holding the opposite opinion.

Even the pessimist will concede that many things today are better than they were in the past. For example, not many pessimists, if they ever became seriously ill, would view the medical advances of recent centuries as so insignificant that they would happily be treated without antibiotics and anaesthesia. Few of them would claim to be especially drawn to the idea of society reverting to women not having the right to vote and slavery being considered an unproblematic institution. If the pessimist has stayed reasonably updated, they will also have noticed that in recent decades we have reduced the proportion of poor, starving, illiterate people on the globe. We are older, richer, freer, more peaceful and better educated than at any other time in history. Each of these points can be met with counterexamples, of people who die young, are poor, unfree, at war and uneducated. The benefits are obviously not equally distributed among the people. Nevertheless, it should be pointed out that an increasingly large proportion of the world's population has gained significantly better living conditions. The pessimist, however, will not necessarily be moved a great deal by such facts. Because the pessimist has their own facts, such as that climate change is changing living conditions on the planet for the worse, that in absolute numbers there have never been more slaves in the world than now, that water supplies are precarious in many places, that COVID-19 may turn out to have been a light pandemic compared to those that are sure to come, that there are still enough nuclear weapons to destroy humanity several times over, that we don't stand a chance if a huge meteorite hits the planet, that the number of liberal democracies has been in decline every single year since 2006, and so on and so forth. A sincere optimist will admit that the pessimist is right about all this but still be able to maintain their optimism.

As mentioned, I consider myself moderately optimistic and fairly hopeful. I used to be far more pessimistic. But to be honest, I don't really know if my past pessimism was always that genuine. It probably was, partly, but it may also have been posing, based on a misunderstood desire to appear 'deep'. According to the scriptures in the Old Testament, early Greek philosophy and Old Norse poetry for that matter, there is a connection between wisdom and pessimism:

> You should be
> only a little wise,
> never too wise.
> A wise man's heart
> is seldom glad
> if he's truly wise.[17]

Maybe wisdom comes with a degree of sadness or melancholy, maybe not. Either way, it doesn't mean you should regard your pessimism as confirmation of your own wisdom. Today, I have more confidence on behalf of the present. But it is a more moderate confidence than the one Kant advocates, for example. As an optimist, and based on my interpretation of history, if we could choose a time in human history to be alive, I would probably consider right now the best choice. That does not mean I am blind to the problems we are facing from poverty, hunger, climate change, epidemics and pandemics, political and religious conflicts and so on. What's needed is a belief in our ability to try to solve these problems step by step, to learn from our mistakes and create a better world. I feel more comfortable with the term 'hopeful' than 'optimistic' because optimism easily switches to being the hubris of hope, where you become overconfident on behalf of the future. Such arrogance can often make one lose sight of the present.

Hope is basically independent of optimism and pessimism. You can be a pessimist and believe things are most likely to go really badly while still hoping for the best and doing your utmost to make it so. Most optimists will probably be hopeful, but the most radical optimists are so convinced of everything going well – of the wonderful future being assured, if not yet realized – that there is no room for hope. Hope exists in the possible, not in the certain. It is only when optimism or pessimism takes on a deterministic or fatalistic form, where everything *must* turn out for the best or the worst respectively, that they no longer contain any room for hope. There is, however, no convincing reason to believe such determinism or fatalism to be true.

When I read the most radical optimists, I often want to swap sides and join the pessimists. They write as if progress is inevitable and that the world can only develop for the better. But there is, of course, no guarantee of that. The future is undetermined. There is a kind of fatalism in the totally certain variant of optimism since it maintains that things cannot fail to go well. As a result, it also implies that optimists are content with what exists since what exists could be no better than it is, and since what exists will be even better in the future. Optimism of this kind will typically lead to one becoming passive, while hope is activistic. Optimism then requires nothing from us in order to create a better world since such a world is already guaranteed, while hope actually *can* demand that we do our utmost to realize something that is only a possibility. Hope is not the opium of the people, but optimism can be precisely that. The optimist who has gone from hope to certainty has at the same time escaped the responsibility of creating a better world for himself and others, because it will inevitably happen anyway.

Both the absolute optimist and the absolute pessimist are certain in a way that appears to be unfounded. They claim to have an overview of the world and history that no human is privileged to. And, as mentioned, hope is not accessible to any of them. Moderate pessimists and optimists accept that our overview is always limited. We can never know the world in its totality, and we do not know how things will turn out. So they can both hope. Whether you end up as a moderate pessimist or a moderate optimist is perhaps mostly a question of intellectual temperament. There are no compelling arguments for one or the other.

A Duty to Optimism?

Like Kant, the Austrian philosopher Karl Popper claims that we have a duty to be optimists:

> It is one's duty to be an optimist. Only from this point of view can one be active and do what one can. If you are a pessimist, you have given up. We must remain optimists, we have to look at the world from the point of view of how beautiful it is, and to try to do what we can to make it better.[18]

However, there is no reason to claim that optimism is linked to activism and pessimism to passivity. Instead, both optimism and pessimism are fully compatible with fervent activism – unless they are absolute – and relate to a future that is open rather than one where the outcome is certain. Both optimism and pessimism, as absolutes, will lead to passivity because their future is certain. Popper's main point is that we have a duty to try to create a better world, and this requires us to believe that creating a better world is possible. He should then have claimed that we have a duty to be hopeful rather than optimistic because such hope is compatible with both optimism and pessimism. The question then is whether it is reasonable to claim that we have a duty to hope.

Since will has very little control over hope, it may seem unreasonable to claim that hoping is a duty. Should presupposes can: there's no certainty that I can hope for something even if I wanted to. Hope is connected to identity, and an identity can oblige you to hope. If my favourite football team plays an important match, my fellow supporters will think I am failing as a supporter if I don't hope our team wins. Had I been alive during the Second World War (and provided I was a 'good Norwegian'), I would have been seen as failing as a patriot if I didn't hope for the German occupiers to be one day driven from the country. If one of my closest friends gets a serious diagnosis, I would, of course, be seriously failing as a friend if I didn't hope that the treatment is successful.

In all these cases we might say that the hope is an almost natural consequence of my identity as a supporter, patriot and friend, respectively. I may be lacking a necessary requirement for hope, namely an ability to see the real possibility of winning the match or the war, or of beating the disease. In that case, I would be seemingly obliged to wish for a positive outcome, even if I am unable to hope for one. The identity itself comes with a certain mindset, and one could even say that part of this mindset is to search for the real possibility. If that is the case, certain identities give one a duty to hope. If I am indifferent, I don't *care* about the football team, the country or the friend, despite pretending to do just that. We might say that I come across as a kind of impostor, pretending to be something I am not. Not caring is incompatible with these roles. The Canadian social scientist Erving Goffman claims that the experience of being deceived is the discovery that a person did not have the right to play the role they had played.[19] In other words, you have the right to play the role of supporter, patriot or friend, but only provided you *are* these things, and if you don't care, you are not a supporter, patriot or friend but simply a fraud pretending to be one. But what if I'm not indifferent, but afraid? It will be more problematic to blame someone who is so overcome by fear that hoping is impossible. Using reason I can see that there is always room for hope, that it is genuinely possible for things to go well, and still not hope, because the fear is so overpowering. Hope and fear don't necessarily follow the dictates of reason. Common sense tells me that I need not fear spiders that are part of Norway's fauna, since none of them are poisonous enough to cause me significant harm, but I can still be terribly afraid of them. The problem is, in short, that fear and hope are not controlled by will.

Can I not train myself to be hopeful? Somewhere along the way I can. I can work on my cognitive and emotional habits to better focus my attention on positive opportunities. But this mastering of thoughts and feelings will only ever be partial, as the Stoic Cicero experienced when his daughter, Tullia, died. Such a dedicated Stoic as Cicero should have handled her death with the greatest equanimity, but he was instead struck by profound grief.[20] He moved away, isolated himself, stopped sleeping and cried endlessly. Other Stoics criticized him for allowing his emotions to afflict him in such a way, telling him that if he was to have any future in politics he needed to regain his self-control. I would argue that Cicero's grief showed that he had a well-functioning emotional life. Ideally the Stoic cares about neither the past nor the future, but tries to relate entirely to the present, and lives an undivided, rational life without allowing himself to be led astray by emotions. Such an ideal comes across as lacking real life. Feeling too much or too little can be a moral flaw. As Aristotle puts it:

For instance, both fear and confidence and appetite and anger and pity and in general pleasure and pain may be felt both too much and too little, and in both cases not well; but to feel them at the right times, with reference to the right objects, towards the right people, with the right aim, and in the right way, is what is both intermediate and best.[21]

Another word for emotions is 'passions', from the Greek word *pathos*, via the Latin *passio*, which describes something that happens to you. In this sense, feelings are something you receive, not something you initiate yourself. One cannot simply choose an emotion. If you're sad or afraid, you can't just choose to have another feeling that makes you feel better. However, we have a certain ability to release an emotion or to suppress it. Aristotle is right about us all being able to work on our emotional lives and shape our emotional dispositions, even if our feelings do not easily conform to our will. To feel the right thing in the right way at the right time is an essential part of being a well-functioning human. To not feel certain things in given situations is to fall short as a moral agent. For example, if you don't feel a hint of anger when you see a person suffer a gross injustice, or a shred of gratitude when someone does you a favour, you are simply not properly emotionally calibrated.

This emotional calibration is something you are partially responsible for. We hold each other and ourselves responsible not only for what we do, but to a certain extent for what we feel and believe. Emotions are not just given, they are something each one of us can work on and modify. Emotions can also be described as habits. By that I'm not saying that they have no biological foundation, just that they are malleable – they can be modified and cultivated. Habits are formed through repetition; they become so integrated into our way of being that they are automated. Hegel refers to habits as a 'second nature', which is a good description since a habit eventually becomes so natural to us that it will seem to have been determined by nature.[22]

There are physical and mental habits. For example, hitting a tennis ball a certain way and reacting angrily when it goes out can both be described as habits. I could hit the ball differently and I could react differently to it going out. Both can be changed, but it requires practice. Similarly, you can also train yourself to hope. Hope is an activity, something we do, not just something that happens to us. You can teach yourself to feel and think better, and this is something you are especially capable of when life puts you to the test, when your thinking and emotional habits collide with reality.

The Australian musician Nick Cave writes:

> Hope and optimism can be different, almost oppos- ing, forces. Hope rises out of known suffering and is the defiant and dissenting spark that refuses to be extinguished. Optimism, on the other hand, can be the denial of that suffering, a fear of facing the darkness, a lack of awareness, a kind of blindness to the actual. Hope is wised-up and disobedient. Optimism can be fearful and false. However, there exists another form of optimism, a kind of radical optimism. This optimism has experienced the suffer- ing of the world, believes in the insubordinate nature of hope and is forever at war with banal pessimism, cynicism and nihilism.[23]

Cave's 'radical optimism' has taken everything that indicates otherwise into account: that things don't always go as we wish and that life can put us through terrible trials that can seem impossible for us to overcome, trials that will define who we are for the rest of our lives. In another text, he elab- orates, pointing out how, when younger, he was the very representative of pessimism, cynicism and nihilism, and was so precisely because he lacked experience and insight. What changed him was the loss of his fifteen-year-old son, Arthur, who fell off a cliff and died. It was that crushing experience that showed him how precious life is and taught him hope. Such hopefulness 'makes demands upon us' where cynicism demands nothing of us: 'It says the world and its inhabitants have value and are worth defending. It says the world is worth believing in.'[24] It is a hope that, at its core, has a belief that there is something in this life worth fighting for, and it is only worth fighting for if the fight can somehow make a difference, if the future is at least partly open.

If there really is an obligation to hope, the question is: an obligation towards whom? The closest answer is: yourself. Hope is an obligation because it is a condition for living a life that is genuinely worth living. You owe it to yourself.

TEN

Losing Hope

The phrase 'while there's life there's hope' originates from the Greek poet Theocritus.[1] He writes that only the dead are without hope, which isn't exactly correct because there can also be life without hope. The question is whether we can describe such a life as a fully *human* life. In Heraklion, Crete, the headstone of the Greek writer Nikos Kazantzakis is inscribed with the words 'I hope for nothing. I fear nothing. I am free.' That Kazantzakis neither hopes nor fears is plain to see, since he is, of course, dead. But whether he can be described as free for that reason is more doubtful.

Based on the word's origin, a person without hope is 'desperate' (from the Latin *desperatio*, which is made up of *de*, 'without', and *spes*, 'hope'). Today this is not how the term 'desperate' is normally used; it instead describes a kind of hyperactive hope that has run wild and a person who is clinging to every possibility. If, as a parent, I were to lose my small child in a large crowd and end up running around desperately trying to find them, one cannot say that I am without hope. I am instead in a frantic state where the hope of finding the child has filled my entire consciousness. In this sense, being desperate is the opposite of being without hope. A desperate person doesn't necessarily act rationally but rather satisfies the criteria for being hopeful. While frantically searching for my child without success, desperation can turn into panic. We can say, most formulaically, that if you remove hope from desperation, you are left with panic.[2] Where hope goes beyond the situation one is in, with a view that it can be exceeded, panic locks a person into a now where he either becomes paralysed or more or less loses control. With desperation there is still rational agency, even if it's not necessarily working optimally, but with panic, it has broken down. A panic-stricken person has lost the ability to orientate themselves in the world. They have also lost themselves.

Hope is a constituent part of my identity. It is hard to imagine what kind of identity I would have if I eliminated all hope from my consciousness. I would come across as a kind of empty 'nobody'.

Heidegger and Bollnow: Hope as a Mood

We should also state the difference between transcendental and empirical hope. 'Transcendental' denotes a condition of possibility, so a transcendental hope will mean a certain orientation to the world that enables specific hopes. We can perhaps also describe transcendental hope as what the German philosopher Martin Heidegger calls a mood. A mood is more general than a feeling – it relates to your experience as a whole, whereas a feeling will normally be directed at one or more specific, intentional objects. In the mood of hope, you are orientated to the world as a whole as a place where there is something to hope for, where hope is possible. Usually feelings are also more fleeting, while moods persist for longer periods. Moods are, according to Heidegger, 'the basic way in which we are *outside* ourselves'.[3] Rather than being a purely subjective phenomenon, they open the world up to us in different ways. Mood presents the world as something that contains meaning. Without mood you would have no reason to orientate yourself towards one thing instead of another, because an absence of mood would also be an absence of meaning. Some moods, such as joy, present a world almost overflowing with meaning, while other moods, such as boredom, present a world where meaning is noticeably absent. In any case, moods open frames of experience, and different moods will open different frames.[4] You must be hopefully inclined in order to find that the world offers room for hope. When you are in a given mood, the world looks like a specific field of possibilities. Different moods enable different relationships to the world as a whole, to objects and to other people. We are essentially passive towards moods. We can make ourselves aware of a mood we are in, but we cannot immediately decide to replace this mood with another. As Heidegger puts it, you can't put a mood on or take one off like a pair of gloves.[5] In that sense, you are at the mercy of the mood. Heidegger writes that we should try to master our moods, but you will search in vain for enlightening descriptions about how this control might be achieved.[6] He implies that we must somehow be able to go into a counter-mood but says nothing about *how* this should be done.[7]

Heidegger writes little about hope, but he has a brief discussion in *Being and Time* (1927):

> In contrast to fear which is related to a *malum futurum*, hope has been characterized as the expectation of a *bonum futurum*. But what is decisive for the structure of hope as a phenomenon is not so much the 'futural' character of that to which it is related as the existential meaning of *hoping itself*. Here, too, the mood character lies primarily in hoping as *hoping something for oneself*. One who hopes takes oneself, so to speak, *along* in the hope and brings oneself toward what is hoped for. But that presupposes having-achieved-oneself. The fact that hope *brings relief* from depressing apprehensiveness only means that even this attunement remains related to a burden in the mode of having-been. Elevated or

elevating moods are ontologically possible only in an ecstatic-temporal relation of Dasein to the thrown ground of itself.[8]

This rather cryptic passage needs explaining. To begin with, Heidegger somewhat imprecisely describes the standard understanding of hope as waiting for a future good, but stresses that he wants to explore the phenomenon more deeply, where the crucial factor will not be what hope is aimed at but what the very act of hoping is. He goes on to claim that hope should be regarded specifically as a mood.

According to Heidegger, our way of being in time is characterized by the fact that we have a relationship with our past and our future, and that we are in the world in a present that also contains the other two aspects of time. We hope in the present but what we hope for will inevitably be co-determined by what has been. What Heidegger calls 'facticity' refers to us being thrown into a situation before there is anything at all we can do. We are thrown into the world and assigned a certain role, certain conditions and so on. This is what is meant by 'thrownness'. We are always already in one situation or another; the world has always already been given to us. We register this through feelings and moods. Hope does not mean waiting passively but rather involves the active anticipation of the future. This is why Heidegger writes that a hopeful person brings themself *towards* what's being hoped for.

Hope otherwise is conspicuously absent from Heidegger's thinking – or rather, the expression 'hope' is conspicuously absent. When Heidegger describes our being, he stresses that it is always 'being-possible', where we are actively projecting towards the future, towards the different possibilities of being.[9] But the possibility of being one rather than the other is precisely why it is considered a form of hope.[10]

The German existential philosopher and educator Otto Friedrich Bollnow criticizes Heidegger for basing his whole philosophy on a single mood, namely anxiety.[11] Heidegger, for his part, claimed that no one had misunderstood *Being and Time* more than Bollnow.[12] Against Bollnow, one can object that he is guilty of a similarly unreasonable privileging of hope. Heidegger claims that care (*Sorge*) is the fundamental structure of our being in the world. Bollnow claims, on the other hand, that hope is more fundamental than care and that only hope can give us any kind of genuine understanding of what care is about. In hope we encounter 'the innermost center of humanity', he writes.[13] I wouldn't go that far because there are several fundamental phenomena in human life, and one could just as rightly claim that fear is equally fundamental. For my part it's not so important to decide on what's most fundamental or whether there are several equally fundamental phenomena, since neither one can be derived from the other.[14]

Bollnow draws a sharp distinction between the individual hopes, which can be imagined and occur in a variety of ways next to each other, and the state of being hopeful, which has no corresponding object.[15] This is a distinction between an intentionally determined feeling and an intentionally undetermined mood. The individual hope is something that can be fulfilled or disappoint precisely because it is aimed at something specific in the world, an event or subject-matter. The mood of hope, on the other hand, is aimed at the world as a whole, as a place where one actually *can* hope. This mood can also be lost, and it is something far more all-encompassing than the loss of an individual hope.

Bollnow describes the future for the person hoping as something that appears to 'helpfully meet humanity and not allow it to crash into the great nothing'.[16] The point is that hope – even if it's directed at something you can't quite see, a possible future – puts solid ground under your feet. It gives you confidence in life and makes action possible. Therefore, he writes, hope is 'the ultimate condition for life'.

Losing Specific Hope and Losing All Hope

Hope can appear on two levels and it can be lost on two levels. We ought to distinguish between losing specific hopes and losing the ability to hope: In the first instance, you may lose one or more hopes. This might be because you realize that what you are hoping for is unlikely to come true. You still *wish* it were possible but you've lost faith in it. Another possibility is that you lose hope because you have evolved. Throughout life we acquire new objects of desire and discard the old ones. Ultimately you can lose all hope such that you no longer know what to hope for. This could, for example, apply to people living in circumstances where the normal objects of desire become pure figments of the imagination. Stories from prisoners in Nazi concentration camps and communist gulags are extreme examples of this. But even if you have lost all hope, as there are no objects of hope visible to you, it doesn't necessarily mean you have lost the ability to hope. In the second instance, you can lose all hope, in that life does not even seem to offer the possibility of hoping for anything. Hope here has been eroded because you no longer see the future as a field of possibilities. So your thoughts, feelings and actions will no longer be able to direct you towards any goal because you have no goal. You are completely trapped in a now without an outside. You have lost the ability to hope. One can lose all hopes without having lost all hope, in the sense that one finds nothing worth hoping for although the ability to hope is still present.

The Italian writer and chemist Primo Levi describes Auschwitz, where he was a prisoner for eleven months until the camp's liberation on 27 January 1945, as a place where hope was impossible:

> Because one loses the habit of hoping in the Lager, and even of believing in one's own reason. In the Lager it is useless to think, because events happen for

the most part in an unforeseeable manner; and it is harmful, because it keeps alive a sensitivity which is a source of pain, and which some providential natural law dulls when suffering passes a certain limit.[17]

Still, it is clear that Levi wasn't entirely without hope in the camp. He also writes about how, when things were at their worst, he retained a 'last senseless, crazy, residue of unavoidable hope'.[18] He hoped to survive the winter, to get hold of something edible or something that could be exchanged for something else to help him survive. His descriptions of daily life in the camp are not characterized by resignation, but by small projects, attempts to exploit opportunities to keep him one step away from doom, and all these projects imply hope. He doesn't talk about hoping for a life beyond the camp – such a possibility was unthinkable for him under the circumstances in which he was living, but there were smaller hopes from day to day. Not all of the prisoners were able to hope. Levi describes those who were called *Muselmänner*:

> Their life is short, but their number is endless. They, the 'Muselmänner', the drowned, form the backbone of the camp, an anonymous mass, continually renewed and always identical, of non-men who march and labor in silence, the divine spark dead within them is already to empty to really suffer. One hesitates to call them living. One hesitates to call their death 'death,' in the face of which they have no fear, as they are too tired to understand.[19]

These people have lost their humanity, their capacity for genuine action after being broken down by inhumane living conditions. They have lost their ability to hope as they mechanically perform small tasks, from moment to moment, until they are no longer able to even do that. Levi, on the other hand, constantly sees small opportunities to make life slightly more bearable.

That one can lose specific hope is uncontroversial. We have all experienced not only that our hope turned to shame, because what we hoped for didn't happen, but that our hope ended before the outcome was settled. The reason for this change may be that one starts to consider the likelihood of the hope being fulfilled as significantly lower, but also that one no longer finds what one hoped for worth hoping for; that the object of the hope has lost its value. For example, you can imagine being a soldier in a war but see that the prospects for victory are so diminished that you lose hope. Or you may find that the cause you are fighting for is no longer worth fighting for because you realize that it isn't a *just* cause. One can also imagine being in such a desperate situation, and so unable to see any happy outcome, that you don't know what to hope for. One's hope finds no ground on which to stand. Nevertheless, your basic capacity for hope can be intact because you are still orientating yourself to the world as if there might be something that your hope can latch onto.

One can also lose this orientation towards reality and, as a result, lose the ability to hope as well. It can also happen in less dramatic circumstances, where the external conditions for hope seem normal.[20] This can apply to people suffering from severe clinical depression. It is well documented that there is a negative correlation between hope and depressive symptoms.[21] People who have previously had clinical depression are less hopeful than people who have never had depression and are more hopeful than those who have clinical depression. At the extreme end there can be people who experience no hope at all; people who know that there is a future, and that time will continue, but see it as a future without significant possibilities.

This kind of hopelessness would also be characteristic of existential boredom. Depression and existential boredom are related phenomena, but it seems possible to establish a distinction between them through the concept of meaning in life: changes in the experience of boredom can be predicted from changes in the experience of meaning in life, but it is not possible to make corresponding predictions from experienced meaning in life to experienced depression.[22] It tells us little about how boredom and meaning in life should be connected, whether less experienced meaning in life creates greater boredom or vice versa.

As I already highlighted, hope is about a future where possibilities can be realized. What is characteristic of existential boredom is that these possibilities do not form part of one's experience. According to Fernando Pessoa, it is 'to suffer without suffering, to want without desire, to think without reason'.[23] With existential boredom the world appears empty – not of objects and events, but of relevant possibilities. Kierkegaard describes it similarly: 'I lie prostrate, inert; the only thing I see is emptiness, the only thing I live on is emptiness, the only thing I move in is emptiness. I do not even suffer pain.'[24] In such a state, one is trapped by a present that is devoid of meaning. Kierkegaard describes boredom as a 'demonic pantheism'.[25] The demonic part is the emptiness, so boredom is then to be understood as a nothingness that permeates all of reality. You simply cannot find anything to care about. It is telling that in Greek antiquity this condition was given the name *akedia*, which later became the Latin *acedia*, which was one of the seven deadly sins.[26] The term *akedia* is a combination of *kedos*, which means to care, and a negative prefix. Quite literally, it means not caring about anything. Your life might develop in such a way that you don't feel like there is anything to care about, regardless of whether the cause is internal or external. You will then have no hope. But you can still hope to find something to hope for.

Radical Hope

You can care about not finding anything to care about. The American philosopher and psychoanalyst Jonathan Lear writes about what he calls 'radical hope': 'Radical hope anticipates a good for which those who have the hope as yet lack the appropriate concepts with which to understand it.'[27] He asks if such hope can be justified. It is about hope, but one where the person hoping basically has no idea what he is hoping for. In that sense, it is a more indefinite hope than the one Paul describes in Romans (4:18), where it is said: 'Against all hope, Abraham in hope believed,' meaning that even though all human hope was gone he could still hope in God. In the philosophical and psychological literature, 'hope against hope' is not necessarily linked to hope in God. To hope against hope is to hope even if one is unable to imagine precisely how the hope might be realized. You can hope for anything, no matter how unlikely, as long as it's not impossible. Lear's radical hope is not only about not knowing how a hope can be realized, but about not even knowing what to hope for.

Lear's example is a Native American who has witnessed the destruction of his entire culture. It is about going on living when what gives life meaning – in fact, the whole framework determining what gives life meaning – has been erased. The life of the tribe had been organized around hunting and war, but it was no longer possible to continue hunting and being at war. The life they knew was irretrievably over. Where would they go from there? One might imagine plenty of other meaningful activities they could do, such as cooking. However, cooking was only meaningful when associated with hunting and war, to give strength to these activities, and now its purpose was gone.[28]

Lear describes a collective loss of hope for an entire tribe, but such losses can also be highly individual. Consider, for example, someone who has organized their entire life around becoming a world-class guitarist or tennis player, and that every important hope they have is linked to either of these things, but that the person in question then loses their arm in a road accident. It would, of course, be a tremendous loss. Some would manage to pin their hopes on something else in life, but it's easy to imagine a situation similar to the one Lear's Native American is in; where one no longer knows what to hope for, since all the hopes were linked to what's now been lost. Even if the specific hopes are lost, one can still relate to the world as somewhere one can hope, where one can hope to be able to hope again.

Lear says that radical hope is the answer, a hope for 'the bare possibility that, from this disaster, something good will emerge', but where it is completely open why and how this indeterminate good will arise.[29] Lear mentions one possibility, namely that the tribe can get a 'new poet' who can show the tribe new ways to live, rather than indulging in nostalgia about what the tribe has been.[30] For me, it would be more appropriate to describe this as a hope that someone will come and convince the Native American of what he should hope for. In other words, it is more of a hope for hope than a hope for something that cannot be conceptualized.

I believe Lear is on the trail of something we may well call radical hope but that he misidentifies the phenomenon. The British philosopher Matthew Ratcliffe argues that instead of being a new hope that appears when all specific hopes are impossible, it is a pre-intentional orientation towards the world or an 'existential feeling'.[31] By 'existential feeling' he means a background orientation that structures our experience as a whole, but we can nevertheless have a bodily awareness of it.[32] This is basically the same as what Heidegger and Bollnow described as hope as a mood. It is about the mere ability to hope, an orientation towards a world where hope is possible. The American theologian and philosopher Joseph Godfrey also uses something he calls 'fundamental hope', which is 'a hope without a goal, which is a tone or a basic disposition with which one faces the future'.[33] But he cannot be said to have developed this concept with impeccable clarity. Such hope can be called 'radical hope' because it is the very root of all other hope, in that the word 'radical' is derived from the Latin *radix*, which means 'root'. What characterizes Lear's Native American, then, is that he hasn't lost his overall ability to hope, to see the future as a field of good opportunities, even though he cannot imagine exactly what these opportunities are.

While Lear believes that radical hope is something that can *arise* in certain existential limit situations, I would argue that it is something that is normally always there, but which can become more apparent in such situations. This hope is more like something we live in than something we focus our attention on. It is a specifically Heideggerian mood. We can make ourselves aware of this mood, and this will typically happen when our attention is not entirely occupied by intentional feelings. When you hope for something specific, this hope fills your attention, but when you are missing something to hope for, the actual capacity to hope can present itself to you. In other words, the absence of specific hopes will reveal a more fundamental capacity for hope that enables specific hopes. I may have exhausted all the imaginable possibilities without finding a way out of my situation, and as such have no specific hope. Nevertheless, I can be hopeful in the sense that my overall hope is intact and I can still see the future as a field of possibilities, even if I cannot now imagine exactly what those possibilities would be.

The Christian existentialist Gabriel Marcel writes about a hope that rises to such a level that it is immune to all disproof.[34] The context is that a loved one suffers from an incurable disease. The reasoning he offers is that it is unthinkable, impossible, that life can be indifferent towards someone that means so much to him. With so much at stake the situation forces you to hope even if there are no realistic grounds for it. This is why it also becomes immune to disproof. It is quite possible that such hope can be comforting, but it is totally irrational. If one is to hope well and reflectively, one must always be open to objections. What Marcel describes here is wishful thinking rather than hope. However, there may be another type of hope that cannot be disproved by specific circumstances without it being irrational for that reason. The usual hope is object-orientated, and it must therefore be possible for it to be disproven by its object, but there is also a more general hope that has no object and which therefore cannot be disproven by any object either. This is not a hope that grows from the specific hopes but is instead what makes hope possible in the first place.

As pointed out, we should therefore distinguish between two levels of hope since there is specific hope, directed at all kinds of desired events, and a more fundamental hope that opens one up to a relationship with the world where there can be something to hope for. It is akin to the distinction between fear and anxiety. Both contain an imagined threat, but this threat can be specific or more undetermined. Fear has a specific object, while anxiety lacks one. In philosophy this distinction is usually associated with Kierkegaard and Heidegger, but Kant anticipates it: 'Fear concerning an object that threatens an undetermined ill is *anxiety*.'[35] The decisive factor is the uncertainty. Correspondingly the specific hopes will be directed towards a specific event that one wants to occur, while the fundamental hope appears to be objectless because it is directed towards the world as a whole. The fundamental hope opens the world up as a place where there is something to hope for.

In *Tractatus logico-philosophicus* (1921) Wittgenstein writes: 'The world of the happy man is a different one from that of the unhappy man.'[36] Similarly we could say that the world of the optimist differs from that of the pessimist and that the hopeful live in a different world from those without hope. They do this despite being related to the same environment, agreeing on the same objective facts and so on. It is natural to say that the difference between the people in one or the other category is that they are differently attuned. Mood creates a basic frame of understanding and experience, so that after a change of mood you *see* a different world even if you are looking at the same world. A mood change like this can happen over time, but it can also happen suddenly. The Swiss psychiatrist Ludwig Binswanger begins his essay on dreams and existence by pointing to the experience of being in a state of profound hope before what we were hoping for turns out to be illusory. What then happens is that the world suddenly looks completely different – our footing in the world has been lost.[37]

E. M. Cioran writes in *A Short History of Decay* (2010) about how he has paradoxically lost the very capacity for hope but clings to a few hopes nevertheless.[38] This is clearly not possible. Specific hopes obviously require a capacity for hope, but it's possible that Cioran just means that his capacity is approaching zero. In *The Trouble with Being Born* (1998) he claims that even if you have revealed the hope for what it is, it isn't possible to live with no hope whatsoever – there will always be an unconscious hope making up for all the hopes you reject or exhaust.[39] Where there is life there will always be hope, he seems to think. He writes that to live is to hope and believe, but that this means lying to oneself.[40] A truly clear vision would reveal that there is nothing to hope for.

But there is, of course, plenty to hope for. The question is not whether there is anything to hope for but rather what one should hope for, and how.

ELEVEN

Hope and Meaning in Life

Hope gives an experience of meaning. Hope can give meaning during life, even if it ultimately ends up unfulfilled. Suppose I dedicate my entire career to developing a cure for cancer – it becomes my life project. My deep involvement would undoubtedly give me a sense of a meaningful existence. Let's say, however, that my approach turns out to be a dead end and that my project ultimately fails. This would be a huge disappointment, of course, but it wouldn't erase the meaning I had experienced along the way. Perhaps even in defeat I might find some satisfaction in the thought that I acted whole-heartedly, that I gave the project everything I had to offer. Hope, by definition, carries no guarantees that things will go as you wish, but it gives life direction; it moves you forward.

Camus, the Absurd and Hope

That human life is 'absurd' is not a conclusion in Albert Camus' investigation of the possibility of a meaningful life, but instead a premise he lays as a basis.[1] He also understands that there is no proof of this premise being true beyond what people might recognize from their own lives. In fact it's not entirely clear what exactly his thesis on the absurd is all about. Camus also seems to think that the experience of the absurd will vary from person to person, but he at least implies that human life does not contain any unconditional meaning, a higher purpose that can justify it all. The absurd then lies in the fact that man demands an unconditional meaning that he can never get from his surroundings. An objection can then be that perhaps a conditional meaning can be enough to live with and live for. Camus writes: 'There is so much stubborn hope in the human heart. The most destitute men often end up accepting illusion.'[2] When hope is so stubborn, it is precisely because it is a crucial part of human agency, but all hope is not illusory. Hope can be attached to something less than the unconditional that Camus demands.

Camus advocates what he calls 'revolt' rather than hope: 'It is not aspiration, for it is devoid of hope. That revolt is the certainty of a crushing fate, without the resignation that ought to accompany it.'[3] The absurd means living with uncertainty, without guarantees, without absolutes. I can agree with this – that they are the parameters for human life – but I still do not consider them at all 'absurd'. The first problem is that Camus is unable to free himself from the idea of some definitive justification of life, in the form of a deity or a historical endpoint, and his philosophy becomes too much of a lament for its absence. Second, he has a rather primitive understanding of hope as being synonymous with resignation or not taking responsibility for one's own life.[4] For Camus the hopeful is someone who loses themselves passively in the future rather than assisting the future in the only possible way, namely by devoting themselves wholeheartedly to the present. One can object that such a wholehearted commitment in the present must necessarily point to the future, towards something one wants to achieve by what one is doing, with no guarantee of success. And what is that, but hope? Camus' position is that this world, with all its imperfections, is all we have, and what we can accomplish in this world is limited, but it is from these limits and imperfections that a meaningful life can arise. This is all overlooked by those who lose themselves hoping for future perfection in this life and the next. I find this hard to disagree with, but it is also what I would consider the framework for secular hope.

Hope is not the same as wishful thinking, because the object of hope must be realizable. Hope is directed towards the real world, not a dreamworld. It is not only about calculating possibilities but about creating these possibilities through action. Meaning is not just something that is given to you but something that you create by participating in the world with all its limitations. Hope is only possible if existence, on some level, has meaning. But it is crucial to see that meaning in life is only possible if there is hope.

Zapffe, the Meaning Denier

To claim that life is simply devoid of meaning is extraordinary. It can, of course, feel meaningless now and then, and if you are struck by deep, existential boredom, life's meaning will have struck rock bottom. But it is quite different to claiming that life is by nature meaningless, as, for example, the Norwegian philosopher Peter Wessel Zapffe does. Zapffe approaches from a biological perspective where all life is seen 'as the tension between task and ability, the struggle of organisms to realize their interests, each in their own environment'.[5] Most living things can, in principle, find this accord between task and ability. Humans are distinguished by having interests that cannot possibly be realized but cannot simply be abandoned either. The problem with the human organism is that it is so 'over-equipped' that it cannot find its place in nature. Even though we are created by nature, we do not fit into it. In the case of humankind, evolution has failed. We have been given abilities that surpass what nature can offer us and are therefore doomed to be unhappy. Man's understanding of himself and the world is precisely what makes him a being that does not fit into the world. He has a need for meaning and justice that can never be satisfied. Man requires:

a world order where everything has its place, a plan and meaning, where suffering, if necessary, is employed according to an economic principle, where destinies are adequate to needs, in short, where everything is fair according to each individual's assessment or according to an assessment that everyone can 'rise to' by themselves.[6]

Such an imagined world order stands in stark contrast to the real world in which man has to live.

Zapffe believes it is metaphysics, which is our over-armament, that makes life impossible.

We place the *metaphysical* demand on life . . . that life should be brimming with meaning, with all that is going on, with all the experienced awareness that we have, which we find irreplaceable, and which constitutes the uniqueness of our being, our solitary chance in world history, our pride and life's journey.[7]

Zapffe has little faith in hope. His view can be summed up as being that hope is irrational, inevitable and passivating:

Hope, which on the one hand is an indispensable stimulus even for the most honest nature, can on the other hand have a dissolving effect both on the character and on the individual's external establishment in life. More specifically, that the individual will passively and constantly look forward to the possibility that *luck*, i.e. the unexpected occurrence of a favourable external coincidence, will solve its problems, rather than employ its abilities under the given conditions and attempt to exploit them, or bend them to its will.[8]

He seems to think that hope inevitably leads to disappointment: if things don't go as you hoped, you are disappointed, and if things actually do go as you hoped, you are disappointed too.[9] Zapffe ends up giving a resounding NO to human life. It is not about finding meaning in adversity or fighting for a justice that the world doesn't offer us. The answer is not a 'revolt', as Camus advocated, but unconditional capitulation. Zapffe believed that humanity basically has only one sensible option: to stop reproducing and cease to exist as a species.

What might seem like a trivial objection to Zapffe is that life, on the contrary, appears to be immensely meaningful. Not only that, I would argue that Zapffe himself felt similarly, not least about the great outdoors and mountain climbing he cherished so highly. Admittedly what he said was: 'mountaineering is as meaningless as life itself – and thus its magic will never die.'[10] But the climbing was undoubtedly something Zapffe cared about, and what's caring about something if not perceiving it as meaningful?

As a lifelong music nerd, my existence gets a daily boost of meaning from music. I can't explain why music is so important to me, why I care so much about it, but it touches me deeply.

Writing books and reading books also provides me with a continuous source of meaning. This doesn't mean that it's continuously available. Now and then I'll get totally stuck in the middle of working on a book and fail to motivate myself into carrying on. Sometimes I'm unable to find a single book that engages me as a reader. But I've been writing books for so many years now that I stay calm and tell myself that the motivation will, of course, return, and that for the time being I should do something else. Playing with or cuddling my dog is something else that I find meaningful, as well as travelling and experiencing new places with my family. Most important of all is everyday life with them. I find all these things immensely meaningful. They are things I really care about – or love, if you will.

Set against a sense of meaning in life such as this, claims about the meaninglessness of life appear odd. It seems to me that meaning deniers such as Zapffe are asking an additional question that is not just about experienced meaning in life, but about the meaning of this meaning. It is a question of a kind of meta-meaning. I doubt if this additional question makes any sense at all. More precisely: it's basically a question where you don't know what an answer could be.

I too can imagine myself thinking that it is 'meaningless' that I have to die, that all the experiences I have had in my life will come to nothing, that everyone I love will die, that absolutely every trace of humanity and everything else living and non-living will be wiped out one day. However, I don't believe that it invalidates the meaning we experience while we are actually living.

Hope gives meaning. Does the meaning disappear if the hope is not fulfilled? Not really; it was experienced as meaningful along the way. Admittedly, the meaning is less than if the hope had succeeded, but the meaning that was there was actually there.

Hope as a Narrative

The problem for meaning deniers like Zapffe is that they cannot find a whole that gives meaning to the parts, even though they could perhaps admit that at least some of the parts can give a semblance of meaning. I would claim that many of the parts are meaningful, and further, that these parts can be placed in a larger context which is life itself. They make up a kind of narrative – along with the meaningless parts that also comprise the narrative. Hope helps to bind life together into a whole because it connects the future with the present.

Is life a narrative governed by hope? The British philosopher Galen Strawson claims that we do not need to perceive human life as a narrative. He distinguishes between 'diachronic' and 'episodic' experiences of the self, where in the latter case one does not regard oneself as someone who was there in the distant past and will be there in the distant future.[11] Furthermore he claims that he himself is an example of someone with episodic experience. His assertion is not that he lives with an experience of a self entirely without a past and future, limited to isolated moments. It is closer to a self that only relates to a recent past and future. He writes: 'I have absolutely no sense of my life as a narrative with form, or indeed as a narrative without form. Absolutely none. Nor do I have any great or special interest in my past. Nor do I have a great deal of concern for my future.'[12] Of course, Strawson isn't denying that he actually has a more distant past and future, that he was born and that he must die, that his past has shaped his present – that he became a philosopher is hardly independent of the fact that his father was one of the last century's best-known British philosophers – and that what he does now sets the stage for what he will do in the future. The point is that he does not experience his life as a coherent – or incoherent – narrative, and that his attention is essentially directed towards the projects he is currently working on.

I find it hard to imagine a person who never experiences the self diachronically – and even harder one who never experiences it episodically – and Strawson himself emphasizes that the diachronic and the episodic are not thought of as absolutes.[13] In *Things That Bother Me* (2018), however, he quotes from his diary and describes something that must be said is a radically episodic experience of the self:

No sense of narrative or development in my life. I don't have any real sense that my life extends beyond the moment – that I am a continuing person from day to day. This was always partly true but I think it has deepened considerably. What continue from day to day are – problems, things to do. They tie my life together. I have no self, really.[14]

Had I not known that this was written by a renowned philosopher, I would have thought that the author was a psychiatric patient with a serious diagnosis, not that I'm going to speculate on which diagnosis would have been the most apt – and for the record, I should add that there can, of course, be renowned philosophers who are also psychiatric patients with serious diagnoses. Alternatively one could say that Strawson's description of himself is reminiscent of Andy Warhol's description of his own film *Kitchen* (1965) as 'illogical, without motivation or character, and completely ridiculous. Very much like real life.'[15] It seems clear that what is described here is quite far from how most people experience their own lives, and quite incompatible with genuine relationships. Strawson's official theory is less radical than the one expressed in his diary, so in what follows I shall assume that the diachronic and the episodic perspectives should not be perceived as absolutes, and that we all would like a degree of both, albeit in varying proportions.

In everyday life, we are for the most part episodic, concerned with individual tasks without explicitly placing them in a larger context, but now and then we see a longer timeline where at least some of the episodes can be arranged in a context that has a narrative structure. Neither the episodic nor the diachronic perspective can be understood without hope, but their hope is different. Episodic hope is more limited, directed at something happening here and now or in the immediate future. Diachronic hope is also directed at what is happening now but as part of the realization of more extensive and distant goals. The episodic person can by all means care about what they do, but it is still not unreasonable to assume that the diachronic perspective has a greater potential for giving life substantial meaning, because the various episodes are bound together into a whole, and this whole can be greater than the sum of its parts.

Strawson argues that episodic people are able to develop and maintain friendships, romantic relationships and loyalties to the same extent as diachronic people since what counts is how we relate to each other in the here and now.[16] For example, you don't need to remember or value previous shared experiences, he writes. In my opinion this is a misunderstanding of what defines such relationships; not in the sense that a friendship or romantic relationship necessarily must – or even should – be primarily devoted to reminiscing about the past, but because the shared history is a component of the relationship. It gets even stranger when you consider the future. With friendship and romantic relationships you mean each other well, and not just in the short term. Episodic people are said to be unconcerned about their own future, and we can assume the same goes for their friend's or lover's future. It would be strange to say to one's friend or lover: 'I don't really care what happens to you in the future.' Part of 'the contract' in such relationships is to hope for the other person: to hope that they will have their hopes fulfilled, even in the future.

But likewise for yourself, it would be strange to not consider life as a kind of whole and see that this whole plays out as a lifecycle. As the French philosopher Paul Ricoeur has pointed out, you can only understand yourself if you are able to tell a reasonably coherent story about who you have been and who you are going to be.[17] It would be more precise to talk about who you hope to become than about who you will become, because who you become is not only dependent on your will. In order to be yourself you must be able to talk about who you have been, who you hope to become and who you are now, between the past and future. The crucial question in this story is: what do you care about?

Our hopes are connected to our practical identity, to our self-understanding and what we find valuable in life. By practical identity I mean the obligations and values that define you as an agent. Another way of putting it is that you are defined by what you care about. The American philosopher Christine Korsgaard writes that your practical identity is 'a description under which you find your life to be worth living and your actions to be worth undertaking'.[18] Can we even imagine a human being having a practical identity without having hope?

What Should You Hope For?

What you should hope for is not given once and for all, since hope needs an orientation towards reality that wishful thinking can do without, and reality changes. Different times give different room for hope. You also change throughout your life, so what you hoped for when you were twelve is hardly the same as what you hope for fifty years later. One can hope for many different things, in many different ways. If I were to be given a serious diagnosis, I would normally hope to be cured. But I can hope for more than that. Serious illness rarely makes us a better version of ourselves – as a rule, we become a worse version, more self-absorbed and less generous – but many people even make it through serious illness without in any way losing character. If I learn that the prognosis is so bad that there's no real chance of recovery, I can hope that the pain will not be too overwhelming and that I will carry on functioning reasonably well for as long as possible. Should the pain become unbearable, I can hope for a speedy end. Hope is a dynamic phenomenon that can constantly change in line with its circumstances.

Hope's range can apply solely to me in that I hope the book I'm writing right now is well received. Its scope can be my family and my friends, or my entire community. In all these cases the hope is connected to something I am involved in.

However, I can also hope for a complete stranger who I have read about in a newspaper, for example. I can hope for people I've never met, like a musician I admire who is in hospital, and I can also feel grief if this musician dies. I can hope for a foreign people, that Ukraine will succeed in resisting the Russian invasion, which is a hope I can have without considering the consequences of the war's outcome for the world situation and thus also for me. Not all interest is self-interest.

There is great variation between us in terms of what we care about and hope for. For example, I can readily admit that I don't hope for any particular football team to win, for the simple reason that I am not the least bit interested in football. What we actually care about varies from person to person, but for most people, this seems to be largely connected to our relationships with a few people. Of course, most of us also care about more than that, and so we should. But is there anything we should *all* care about?

As mentioned, hope is constitutive for your identity. It is difficult to separate who you are from what you hope for. Your identity as a member of a family and a community implies that you should have certain expectations. You will not be a good citizen if you do not hope for the best for your fellow citizens. We can extend this to our identity as a fellow human or to the identification we should have with non-human animals that are capable of feeling and so on. A large amount of hope, spread over a number of different objects, seems to be a necessary condition for being a well-functioning moral agent.

We all seemingly hope for happiness, but we also hope for more than that, at least if we go by the modern understanding of happiness as meaning a sense of well-being. As Nietzsche writes, with a cutting jab at the British utilitarians who regarded happiness to be pleasure and the absence of unpleasure, and who further believed that the moral yardstick for any action is whether it promotes happiness: 'If you have your "why?" in life, you can get along with almost any "how?" People don't strive for happiness, only the English do.'[19] Nietzsche expresses a similar thought in *Thus Spoke Zarathustra* (1883–5): 'I haven't strived for happiness for a long time, I strive for my work.'[20] Happiness, be it approached from a hedonistic, pessimistic, utilitarian or virtue ethical perspective, is, in Nietzsche's opinion, an inadequate measure of life.[21] I wouldn't be so dismissive about happiness being a crucial part of what we can and should strive for, but it is a happiness linked to functioning well as a human being and is not something that can be reduced to just pleasure.

We strive for happiness, but we do it for more than our own benefit, and we strive for more than happiness, namely meaning. I hope that my wife and daughter will be happy, and of course, I am happy that they are happy, but I don't want them to be happy *because* that in turn increases my happiness. I wish them the best of fortune for themselves. I hope I can be of use, that I might contribute a little to making the world better for someone. I hope I will live a good life, and a good life consists of more than well-being. In order for my life to seem justified – to myself, of course – I must accomplish something that has a meaning beyond my subjective satisfaction. I have to care about something other than myself. As philosopher John Stuart Mill correctly points out: 'When people who are tolerably fortunate in their outward lot do not find in life sufficient enjoyment to make it valuable to them, the cause generally is, caring for nobody but themselves.'[22]

There isn't only one absolute good that is good in its own right and not just because it contributes to the realization of a greater good. A good life can be realized in so many ways, without any definitive common norm. Many very different good lives are possible. Hope obligates, and obligations are what most fundamentally give life meaning. What you hope for will be an expression of your values, of what you consider to be valuable. So what should you care about? I cannot answer that question for you. There is no indisputable, neutral zero point from which all values can be derived. This applies not only to values but to all knowledge. You can examine your beliefs about facts in more detail – criticize, modify, defend or reject them – just as you do with your values. You can only do that based on other perceptions and values that you already have, and that are put into play when you make new experiences.

The Humility of Hope

To live well one must be able to handle the trials that life inevitably presents. Hope helps us with that. Those who hope will often fantasize, imagine things that have not yet occurred and perhaps just might. These imaginings make it easier for us to endure adversity. At the same time, it is crucial that we do not lose ourselves in hope in the sense that we focus so exclusively on the future that we overlook the present.

We have to settle for living with possibilities because life offers no guarantees, except that one day it will end. Death puts an end to my hopes for myself. I can also fantasize about a life in the hereafter, but I cannot see a real possibility of such an existence, so there is no room to hope for it for me. However, I can hope that things will go well for my family and friends after I'm gone. I can hope that humanity will continue to evolve for the better and that the planet will remain habitable. I can also hope to be remembered, at least for a while, so that the traces I leave aren't erased immediately.

Within hope lies humility, an acknowledgement that much of what is of great importance to us in life is beyond our control. We can do our best, and then we can hope. Justice doesn't always prevail, and truth doesn't always overcome lies. Even if we do our very best, we will not always succeed; to believe otherwise is to indulge in self-deception. The fact that things don't always go as we wish is, of course, no argument for not doing our utmost. To believe the opposite, to choose disillusionment as an ideal, is no more rational than indulging in some form of superstition where a divine guarantee or similar is given that truth and justice will prevail. Both of these extremes are without hope – they are characterized by a certainty that things will go well or badly, respectively. So they also overlook that truth and justice are tasks to realize, not just something given to us or denied us. Truth and justice are duties, and we must hope to succeed in realizing them, knowing that we will often fail.

The German philosopher Hans-Georg Gadamer describes hope as 'a fundamental structure in our awareness of life, without which we would hardly be able to carry the burdens of life'.[23] He warns against indulging in an empty hope that makes us passive, but points out that we cannot manage without hope, with no ability to transcend our situation using the power of thought and project towards the future of a better life. Hope can make dealing with life's trials easier because it gives your gaze something to hold on to, somewhere you can put these trials into a larger context. It means you are not entirely at the mercy of the pain you feel here and now.

Hope is, however, more than just a comfort. If you can't imagine being able to do something, you won't be able to do it. In that sense, hope is a requirement for action. If you lose hope, you also lose the ability to act. Towards the end of *Prometheus Unbound* (1820), the British romantic Percy Bysshe Shelley writes: 'to hope till Hope creates/ From its own wreck the thing it contemplates'.[24] Hope is not a mental state that magically changes the world, but it does make you inclined to take action to make that happen. Hope, by definition, gives you no guarantees, but without hope, as we all know, life is hopeless.

References

Unless otherwise indicated, all English translations of original-language works cited in this book are by Matt Bagguley.

Introduction

1 Thucydides, *The Peloponnesian War*, trans. Martin Hammond (Oxford: Oxford University Press, 2009), Book 5.103, p. 304.

2 Ibid., Book 5.116, p. 307.

3 Hesiod, *Works and Days*, trans. Glenn W. Most, in *Theogony/ Works and Days/Testimonia* (Cambridge, MA: Harvard University Press, 2006), verses 90–97. The translation has been modified. The translator has rendered *elpis* as 'anticipation', but I have changed this to the more traditional translation: 'hope'. The meaning of this Greek term will be discussed further in Chapters One and Six.

4 Ibid., verses 498, 500.

5 Friedrich Nietzsche, *Dawn*, trans. Brittain Smith (Stanford, CA: Stanford University Press, 2011), §38.

6 Friedrich Nietzsche, *Human, All Too Human*, trans. R. J. Hollingdale (Cambridge: Cambridge University Press, 1996), part I, §71, p. 68.

7 Ernst Bloch, *The Principle of Hope*, trans. Neville Plaice, Stephen Plaice and Paul Knight, vol. I (Cambridge, MA: MIT Press, 1995), p. 3.

8 This book will primarily discuss the philosophical literature on hope. For readers who also want an overview of the most important psychological perspectives and findings, see Matthew W. Gallagher and Shane J. Lopez, eds, *The Oxford Handbook of Hope* (Oxford: Oxford University Press, 2018).

ONE What Is Hope?

1 Perhaps what was left in Pandora's jar was not what we call
'hope'; *elpis* can have other meanings. It can have the positive
meaning 'expectation' but also more neutral meanings such
as 'preconceptions', or purely negative meanings such as 'mis-
leading expectation'. According to Plato, the object of *elpis*
can be something positive that one desires but also something
negative that one wants to avoid (cf. Plato, *The Laws of Plato*,
trans. Thomas L. Pangle (Chicago, IL/London: University of
Chicago Press, 1988)). In isolation, *elpis* is neither positively
nor negatively charged, but it is usually clear from the context
whether what one is imagining the possibility of is good or
bad. If you wanted to make it clear that it was about hoping
for something positive, you sometimes used the expression
euelpis, which literally means 'hoping for something good'. For
an overview of *elpis* in Greek antiquity, see Douglas Cairns,
'Hope in Archaic and Classical Greek', in Claudia Blöser and
Titus Stahl, eds, *The Moral Psychology of Hope* (London/New
York: Rowman and Littlefield, 2020).

2 Aristotle, *Rhetoric*, trans. W. Rhys Roberts, in *The Complete
Works of Aristotle*, vol. II (Princeton, NJ: Princeton University
Press, 1985), 1370a.

3 Ludwig Wittgenstein, *Philosophical Investigations*, trans.
G.E.M. Anscombe (Oxford: Blackwell, 1967), §545.

4 Cf. Aaron Ben-Ze'ev, *The Subtlety of Emotions* (Cambridge,
MA: MIT Press, 2000).

5 The social anthropologist Paul Ekman claims that there is a
set of 'basic emotions' (Paul Ekman, 'An Argument for Basic
Emotions', *Cognition and Emotion*, VI/3–4 (1992)). By that
he means emotions that people of all cultures have which
are not learned but innate. Although it is conceivable that
such basic emotions exist, there is much disagreement about
which emotions are involved. In a review of fourteen lists of
'basic emotions' it is striking how there is no single emotion
that is present on all of them (cf. Andrew Ortony, Gerald L.
Clore and Allan Collins, *The Cognitive Structure of Emotions*
(Cambridge: Cambridge University Press, 1998), p. 27). Anger,
fear, joy, disgust and surprise are on most of the lists, but
beyond that the lists vary significantly. (For a worthwhile

summary and discussion of the 'basic emotions' debate, see Robert C. Solomon, 'Back to Basics: On the Very Idea of "Basic Emotions"', in *Not Passion's Slave: Emotions and Choice* (Oxford: Oxford University Press, 2003).) All emotions have a natural history, but they are also shaped by a social and a personal history.

6 Katie Stockdale, 'Emotional Hope', in Blöser and Stahl, eds, *The Moral Psychology of Hope*.

7 Cf. Joanna Bourke, *Fear: A Cultural History* (London: Virago, 2005), p. 19.

8 Cf. Ronald de Sousa, 'Self-Deceptive Emotions', in Amélie Oksenberg Rorty, ed., *Explaining Emotions* (Berkeley, CA: University of California Press, 1980), pp. 283–97.

9 Wittgenstein, *Philosophical Investigations*, II.i, p. 174. Cf. Ludwig Wittgenstein, *Remarks on the Philosophy of Psychology*, vol. II (Oxford: Blackwell, 1983), §16.

10 Wittgenstein, *Philosophical Investigations*, §583.

11 I discuss this more extensively in Lars Fr. H. Svendsen, *Understanding Animals: Philosophy for Dog and Cat Lovers*, trans. Matt Bagguley (London: Reaktion Books, 2019), ch. 2.

12 Ernst Cassirer, *An Essay on Man: An Introduction to a Philosophy of Human Culture* (New York: Doubleday, 1954), pp. 42–3.

13 Ludwig Wittgenstein, *Remarks on the Philosophy of Psychology*, vol. I (Oxford: Blackwell, 1983), §15.

14 Ibid., §16.

15 Wittgenstein, *Philosophical Investigations*, II.ix, p. 217.

16 Wittgenstein, *Remarks on the Philosophy of Psychology*, vol. II, §154.

17 Johann Wolfgang von Goethe, *Faust, Part II*, trans. D. Constantine (London: Penguin Books, 2009), verse 5441.

18 Friedrich Schlegel, *Lucinde*, trans. Peter Firchow (Minneapolis, MN: University of Minnesota Press, 1971), p. 57.

19 Ibid., p. 137.

20 Michel de Montaigne, *The Essays of Michel Eyquem de Montaigne*, trans. Charles Cotton (Chicago, IL: Encyclopaedia Britannica, 1952), p. 6.

21 Ibid., p. 426.

TWO Defining Hope

1 René Descartes, *The Passions of the Soul*, in *The Philosophical Writings of Descartes*, trans. John Cottingham, Robert Stoothoff and Dugald Murdoch, vol. I (Cambridge: Cambridge University Press, 1985), pp. 350, 359.

2 Ibid., p. 389.

3 Thomas Hobbes, *Leviathan* (Cambridge: Cambridge University Press, 1991), I.6, pp. 41, 65.

4 John Locke, *An Essay Concerning Human Understanding* (London: Penguin Books, 2004), Book II.xx.

5 David Hume, *A Treatise of Human Nature* (London: Penguin Books, 1984), Book II.iii.ix, p. 431.

6 Viktor Frankl, *Man's Search for Meaning* (New York: Washington Square Press, 1985), p. 103.

7 Cf. Ariel Meirav, 'The Nature of Hope', *Ratio*, XXII/2 (2009).

8 Another approach would be to see hope as a primitive mental state that cannot be analysed in terms of more basic components such as beliefs and desires. Cf. Gabriel Segal and Mark Textor, 'Hope as a Primitive Mental State', *Ratio*, XXVIII/2 (2015).

9 Luc Bovens, 'The Value of Hope', *Philosophy and Phenomenological Research*, LVIII/3 (1999).

10 Philip Pettit, 'Hope and Its Place in Mind', *Annals of the American Academy of Political and Social Science*, DXCII (2004).

11 Adrienne Martin, *How We Hope: A Moral Psychology* (Princeton, NJ: Princeton University Press, 2014), especially ch. 2. Martin took the term 'incorporation thesis' from Henry Allison's interpretation of Kant, which denotes the view that an impulse or drive can determine a person's ability to choose only if the person has chosen to incorporate it into his maxim of action (cf. Henry E. Allison, *Kant's Theory of Freedom* (Cambridge: Cambridge University Press, 1990), p. 40).

12 Cf. Catherine Rioux, 'Hope: Conceptual and Normative Issues', *Philosophy Compass*, XVI/3 (2021); Michael Milona, 'Finding Hope', *Canadian Journal of Philosophy*, XLIX/5 (2019).

13 François de La Rochefoucauld, *Collected Maxims and Other Reflections*, trans. E. H. Blackmore, A. M. Blackmore and Francine Giguére (Oxford: Oxford University Press, 2007), part V, §27.

14 C. R. Snyder, 'The Past and Possible Futures of Hope', *Journal of Social and Clinical Psychology*, XIX/1 (2000).

15 Margaret Urban Walker, *Moral Repair: Reconstructing Moral Relations after Wrongdoing* (Cambridge: Cambridge University Press, 2006), p. 48.

16 Ludwig Wittgenstein, *Philosophical Investigations*, trans. G.E.M. Anscombe (Oxford: Blackwell, 1967), §67ff.

THREE Is Hope Irrational?

1 Friedrich Nietzsche, *The Anti-Christ*, in *The Anti-Christ, Ecce Homo, Twilight of the Idols and Other Writings*, trans. Judith Norman (Cambridge: Cambridge University Press, 2005), §23, p. 19.

2 Friedrich Nietzsche, *Human, All Too Human*, trans. R. J. Hollingdale (Cambridge: Cambridge University Press, 1986), II.i, §320, p. 285.

3 Friedrich Nietzsche, *Daybreak*, trans. R. J. Hollingdale (Cambridge: Cambridge University Press, 1986–97), §206, p. 126.

4 Ibid., §546.

5 Epictetus, *Handbook of Epictetus*, trans. Nicholas P. White (Indianapolis, IN: Hackett, 1983), §8, p. 13.

6 Nietzsche, *Human, All Too Human*, I, §443, p. 163.

7 Ibid., I, §2, p. 12.

8 Ibid., II.ii, §183, p. 354.

9 Friedrich Nietzsche, *Ecce Homo*, in *The Anti-Christ, Ecce Homo, Twilight of the Idols and Other Writings*, p. 99.

10 Ibid., p. 143.

11 Friedrich Nietzsche, *The Gay Science*, trans. Josefine Nauckhoff (Cambridge: Cambridge University Press, 2001), §12.

12 Ibid., §306, p. 174.

13 Ibid., §326, p. 182.

14 Friedrich Nietzsche, *Thus Spoke Zarathustra*, trans. A. Del Caro (Cambridge: Cambridge University Press, 2006), p. 263.

15 E. M. Cioran, *Drawn and Quartered*, trans. Richard Howard (New York: Arcade Publishing, 1998), p. 102. Cf. E. M. Cioran, *A Short History of Decay*, trans. Richard Howard (London: Penguin Books, 2010), p. 102.

16 Cioran, *A Short History of Decay*, p. 47.

17 E. M. Cioran, *On the Heights of Despair*, trans. Ilinca
     Zarifopol-Johnston (Chicago, IL/London: University of
     Chicago Press, 1992), p. 49

18 William Ian Miller, *Outrageous Fortune: Gloomy Reflections on
     Luck and Life* (Oxford: Oxford University Press, 2021), p. 16.

19 There is ample empirical evidence for this. See Matthew W.
     Gallagher and Shane J. Lopez, eds, *The Oxford Handbook of
     Hope* (Oxford: Oxford University Press, 2018).

20 Barbara Ehrenreich, 'Pathologies of Hope', *Harper's Magazine*,
     7 February 2007.

21 Bernard Williams, 'Truth, Politics, and Self-Deception', *Social
     Research*, LXIII/3 (1996), p. 606.

22 Ludwig Wittgenstein, *Philosophical Occasions, 1912–1951,*
     ed. James C. Klagge and Alfred Nordmann (Indianapolis, IN:
     Hackett, 1993), p. 130.

23 Ibid., p. 136.

24 Ludwig Wittgenstein, *Philosophische Grammatik. Werkausgabe
     in 8 Bänden, Band 4* (Frankfurt a.M.: Suhrkamp, 1984),
     p. 227; Ludwig Wittgenstein, *Philosophische Bemerkungen.
     Werkausgabe in 8 Bänden, Band 2* (Frankfurt a.M.: Suhrkamp,
     1984), §26.

25 John Stuart Mill, 'Theism', in *Essays on Ethics, Religion and
     Society* (London: Routledge, 1969), p. 484.

26 David Hume, *Essays: Moral, Political, and Literary*
     (Indianapolis, IN: Liberty Fund, 1985), p. 74.

27 Ibid., p. 167.

28 David Hume, *A Treatise of Human Nature* (Oxford: Clarendon
     Press, 1965), p. 414.

FOUR Hope and Freedom

 1 Baruch Spinoza, *Short Treatise on God, Man, and His Well-
     Being*, in *Complete Works*, trans. Samuel Shirley (Indianapolis,
     IN: Hackett, 2002), p. 74.

 2 Baruch Spinoza, *Ethics and Selected Letters*, trans. Samuel
     Shirley (Indianapolis, IN: Hackett, 1982), IIIP18, p. 116.

 3 Ibid., IIIP50, p. 133.

 4 Ibid., IVP47, p. 175.

 5 I have given a more extensive presentation of my views on
     freedom in Lars Fr. H. Svendsen, *A Philosophy of Freedom*,
     trans. Kerri Pierce (London: Reaktion Books, 2014).

6 Thomas Aquinas, *Summa theologiae*, Treatise on Virtues, Question 67: 'Of the Duration of Virtues after This Life', Article 4, Reply to Objection 2, https://aquinas101.thomistic institute.org, accessed 1 January 2024.

7 Hannah Arendt, *The Human Condition* (Chicago, IL/London: University of Chicago Press, 1958).

8 William James, *The Will to Believe and Other Essays* (New York: Dover Publications, 1956), p. 151.

9 Max Weber, *The Protestant Ethic and the 'Spirit' of Capitalism*, trans. Peter Baehr and Gordon C. Wells (London: Penguin Books, 2002).

10 I have a far more extensive discussion of the relation between freedom and determinism in Svendsen, *A Philosophy of Freedom*, especially part I.

11 Thomas Hobbes, *Leviathan* (Cambridge: Cambridge University Press, 1991), I.6, p. 44.

12 Ibid., I.10, p. 65.

FIVE   The Politics of Hope

1 For the presentation of Spinoza's political philosophy, I'm in great debt to Justin Steinberg, *Spinoza's Political Psychology: The Taming of Fortune and Fear* (Cambridge: Cambridge University Press, 2018).

2 Baruch Spinoza, *Theological-Political Treatise*, trans. Michael Silverthorne and Jonathan Israel (Cambridge: Cambridge University Press, 2007), §1, p. 3.

3 Ibid., §5, p. 5.

4 Baruch Spinoza, *The Political Treatise*, in *The Collected Works of Spinoza*, trans. Edwin Curley, vol. II (Princeton, NJ: Princeton University Press, 2016), III.8, p. 520.

5 Baruch Spinoza, *Ethics and Selected Letters*, trans. Samuel Shirley (Indianapolis, IN: Hackett, 1982), IVP54A, p. 185.

6 Spinoza, *Theological-Political Treatise*, V.9, p. 73.

7 Thomas Hobbes, *On the Citizen*, trans. Richard Tuck and Michael Silverthorne (Cambridge: Cambridge University Press, 1998), p. 111.

8 Thomas Hobbes, *Leviathan* (Cambridge: Cambridge University Press, 1991), II.21, p. 152.

9 Ibid., II.27, p. 206.

10 Spinoza, *Theological-Political Treatise*, verse 6, p. 530.

11 Ibid., VI.1, p. 532.

12 Spinoza writes: 'Now we must consider how this agreement has to be made if it is to be accepted and endured. For it is a universal law of human nature that no one neglects anything that they deem good unless they hope for a greater good or fear a greater loss, and no one puts up with anything bad except to avoid something worse or because he hopes for something better. That is, of two good things every single person will choose the one which he himself judges to be the greater good, and of two bad things he will choose that which he deems to be less bad. I say expressly what appears to him the greater or lesser good when he makes this choice, since the real situation is not necessarily as he judges it to be. This law is so firmly inscribed in human nature that it may be included among the eternal truths that no one can fail to know. It necessarily follows that no one will promise without deception to give up his right to all things, and absolutely no one will keep his promises except from fear of a greater ill or hope of a greater good.' (Spinoza, *Theological-Political Treatise*, XVI.6, p. 198.)

13 Cf. Geoffrey Hosking, *Trust: A History* (Oxford: Oxford University Press, 2014), ch. 1.

14 See, for instance, Karl Schlögel, *Moscow, 1937*, trans. Rodney Livingstone (Cambridge: Polity Press, 2012).

15 Hannah Arendt, *The Origins of Totalitarianism* (San Diego, CA/New York/London: Harcourt Brace and Company, 1979), p. 323.

16 See especially David R. Shearer, *Policing Stalin's Socialism: Repression and Social Order in the Soviet Union, 1924–1953* (New Haven, CT/London: Yale University Press, 2009). Another important source is J. Arch Getty and Oleg V. Naumov, *The Road to Terror: Stalin and the Self-Destruction of the Bolsheviks, 1932–39* (New Haven, CT/London: Yale University Press, 1999).

17 Judith N. Shklar, *Political Thought and Political Thinkers* (Chicago, IL/London: University of Chicago Press, 1998), ch. 1.

18 Ibid., p. 11.

19 Ibid., p. 166f.

20 Francis Herbert Bradley, *Aphorisms* (Oxford: Clarendon Press, 1930), §63.

21 Michael Walzer, 'On Negative Politics', in Bernard Yack, ed., *Liberalism without Illusions* (Chicago, IL/London: University of Chicago Press, 1996).

22 Immanuel Kant, 'An Answer to the Question: "What Is Enlightenment?"', in *Political Writings*, trans. H. B. Nisbet (Cambridge: Cambridge University Press, 1991), p. 54.

23 John Rawls, *The Law of Peoples* (Cambridge, MA: Harvard University Press, 1999), p. 127; John Rawls, *Political Liberalism*, expanded edn (New York: Columbia University Press, 1996), pp. 133–72; John Rawls, *Justice as Fairness: A Restatement* (Cambridge, MA: Harvard University Press, 2001), §59.

24 Rawls, *Political Liberalism*, p. 58.

25 Rawls, *The Law of Peoples*, p. 7.

26 Ibid., p. 23.

27 Ibid., p. 6, n. 8.

28 As even the utopian Karl Marx pointed out in *Critique of the Gotha Program* (1875), one cannot ever create 'full equality', since introducing one form of equality will inevitably give rise to another form of inequality. (Karl Marx, *Critique of the Gotha Program*, in Lawrence H. Simon, ed., *Selected Writings* (Indianapolis, IN: Hackett, 1994).) One cannot, for example, have both full equality of opportunity and full equality of results. Equality of opportunity will inevitably create inequality of results since people will manage their opportunities differently. If one wants to realize equality of results, it therefore presupposes inequality of opportunity – someone must start with an advantage over others if everyone is to end up equal. This does not mean that we should not try to reduce certain forms of inequality, knowing that it will increase certain other forms of inequality, but it must be discussed and assessed on a case-by-case basis. If one were to believe that equality of results is generally more important than equality of opportunity, there will also be limits to which political measures are acceptable.

29 Rawls, *The Law of Peoples*, p. 128.

30 Karl R. Popper, *The Open Society and Its Enemies*, vol. I: *The Spell of Plato* (London: Routledge, 2005), ch. 9.

31 John Dewey, 'Analysis of Reflective Thinking', in *The Later Works*, vol. VIII (Carbondale, IL: Southern Illinois University Press, 1986), p. 201.

32 John Dewey, 'Liberalism and Social Action', in *The Later
Works*, vol. XI (Carbondale, IL: Southern Illinois University
Press, 1987), p. 56.

SIX To Hope Well and to Hope Badly

1 Diogenes Laertius, *Lives of Eminent Philosophers*, trans.
Stephen White (Cambridge: Cambridge University Press,
2020), 5.18, p. 202.
2 Aristotle, *On Dreams*, trans. J. I. Beare, in *The Complete Works
of Aristotle*, vol. I (Princeton, NJ: Princeton University Press,
1985), 459a.
3 Aristotle, *On Divination in Sleep*, trans. J. I. Beare, in *The
Complete Works of Aristotle*, vol. I, 463b.
4 Aristotle, *Sense and Sensibilia*, trans. J. I. Beare, in *The
Complete Works of Aristotle*, vol. I, 449b11f, 449b25ff.
5 Aristotle, *Rhetoric*, trans. W. Rhys Roberts, in *The Complete
Works of Aristotle*, vol. II (Princeton, NJ: Princeton University
Press, 1985), 1370b9f.
6 Aristotle, *Nicomachean Ethics*, trans. W. D. Ross, in *The
Complete Works of Aristotle*, vol. II, 1111b20–25.
7 Ibid., 1100aff.
8 Aristotle seems to view hope as an aspect of fear: 'If they are
to feel the anguish of uncertainty, there must be some expectation of escape. This appears from the fact that fear sets us
thinking what can be done, which of course nobody does
when things are hopeless.' (Aristotle, *Rhetoric*, 1383a5–8.) Here
it must be pointed out that Aristotle is not entirely consistent,
because he also writes that the coward is a person without
hope because he fears everything (Aristotle, *Nicomachean
Ethics*, 1116a). Hope seems to be characterized by an exposure
to risk, but in a way where one is not immobilized and instead
sees opportunities for action. However, Aristotle links hope
not only to fear but to anger; he writes: 'It [anger] must always
be attended by a certain pleasure – that which arises from the
expectation of revenge. For it is pleasant to think that you will
attain what you aim at, and nobody aims at what he thinks he
cannot attain.' (Aristotle, *Rhetoric*, 1378b2f.) Here, hope is not
linked to something negative to be avoided but to something
positive to be achieved.
9 Aristotle, *Rhetoric*, 1380f.

10 Ibid., 1389a.

11 Ibid., 1389b–90a.

12 Ibid., 1390a–b.

13 Aristotle, *Nicomachean Ethics*, 1117a10–15.

14 Ibid., 1116a1–5.

15 Ibid., 1115b3f.

16 Victoria McGeer, 'The Art of Good Hope', *Annals of the American Academy of Political and Social Science*, DXCII (2004).

17 Cf. Luc Bovens, 'The Value of Hope', *Philosophy and Phenomenological Research*, LVIII/3 (1999), p. 680.

SEVEN Eternal and Finite Hope

1 Augustine, *The City of God*, trans. Marcus Dods (New York: Modern Library, 2000), p. 829.

2 Søren Kierkegaard, *Fear and Trembling*, trans. Alastair Hannay (New York: Penguin Books, 2006), p. 134.

3 Søren Kierkegaard, *Sickness unto Death*, trans Howard V. Hong and Edna H. Hong (Princeton, NJ: Princeton University Press, 1980), p. 38.

4 'He still lives in the finite, but he does not have his life in it. His life, just like anyone else's, has the diverse predicates of a human existence, but he inhabits them as one who goes around in clothes borrowed from a stranger. He is a stranger in the world of the finite, but does not define his difference from worldliness by an alien mode of dress (a contradiction, since it would define him as worldly); he is incognito, but his incognito consists precisely in looking just like everyone else.' (Søren Kierkegaard, *Concluding Unscientific Postscript*, trans. Alastair Hannay (Cambridge: Cambridge University Press, 2009), p. 345.)

5 Kierkegaard did not give any comprehensive presentation of his views on hope anywhere in his writings; what we have are separate remarks in various works. There is clearly more to say about his views on hope than what I have covered in these brief remarks on the knight of faith. For a good, broader presentation, see Roe Fremstedal, 'Kierkegaard on Hope as Essential to Selfhood', in Claudia Blöser and Titus Stahl, eds, *The Moral Psychology of Hope* (London/New York: Rowman and Littlefield, 2020).

6 Augustine, *Confessions*, trans. T. Williams (Indianapolis, IN: Hackett, 2019), Book IX.12–13, pp. 158ff.

7 Ibid., p. 160.

8 Ibid., IV.10, p. 51.

9 Ibid., IV.11, p. 52.

10 John Maynard Keynes, *A Tract on Monetary Reform* (Amherst, NY: Prometheus Books, 2000), p. 80.

11 E. M. Cioran, *Drawn and Quartered*, trans. Richard Howard (New York: Arcade Publishing, 1998), p. 152.

12 Aristotle, *Rhetoric*, trans. W. Rhys Roberts, in *The Complete Works of Aristotle*, vol. II (Princeton, NJ: Princeton University Press, 1985), 1382b.

13 Max Brod, *Franz Kafka: A Biography* (New York: Schocken Books, 1960), p. 75.

EIGHT What Can I Hope For? Immanuel Kant and Maria von Herbert

1 Immanuel Kant, *Critique of Pure Reason*, trans. P. Guyer and A. Wood (Cambridge: Cambridge University Press, 1998), pp. A804f, B832f.

2 Johann Wolfgang von Goethe, 'An C.G. Voigt, Weimar 19. Dezember 1798', in Immanuel Kant, *Anthropologie in pragmatischer Hinsicht* (Hamburg: Felix Meiner, 1980), p. 337.

3 Immanuel Kant, *Correspondence*, trans. Arnulf Zweig (Cambridge: Cambridge University Press, 1999), p. 379.

4 Ibid., p. 411.

5 Ibid., p. 450f.

6 Albert Camus, *The Myth of Sisyphus and Other Essays*, trans. Justin O'Brien (London: Penguin Books, 1979), p. 11.

7 Kant, *Correspondence*, pp. 474ff.

8 Cf. Bernhard Ritter, 'Solace or Counsel for Death', in Corey W. Dyck, ed., *Women and Philosophy in Eighteenth-Century Germany* (Oxford: Oxford University Press, 2021), pp. 137–56.

9 Immanuel Kant, *Anthropology from a Pragmatic Point of View*, trans. M. Gregor (The Hague: Nijhoff, 1974), §74, pp. 122, 255.

10 Immanuel Kant, 'On the Common Saying: "This May Be True in Theory, but Does Not Apply in Practice"', in *Political Writings*, trans. H. B. Nisbet (Cambridge: Cambridge University Press, 1991), p. 73.

11 Immanuel Kant, *Critique of the Power of Judgement*, trans.
    P. Guyer and E. Matthews (Cambridge: Cambridge University
    Press, 2002), pp. 301n, 434n. Cf. Immanuel Kant, 'Über das
    Mißlingen aller philosophischen Versuche in der Theodizee',
    in Preußischen Akademie der Wissenschaften, ed., *Kants
    gesammelte Schriften Band 8* (Berlin/New York: de Gruyter,
    1902ff), p. 259.

12 Immanuel Kant, 'Conjectural Beginning of Human History', in
    Anthropology, History, and Education, trans. R. B. Louden and
    G. Zöller (Cambridge: Cambridge University Press, 2007),
    §122, p. 174.

13 Kant, *Critique of Pure Reason*, pp. A809, B837.

14 See especially Immanuel Kant, *Critique of Practical Reason*,
    trans. M. Gregor (Cambridge: Cambridge University Press,
    2015), pp. 98–107, 122–34.

15 Immanuel Kant, *The Metaphysics of Morals*, trans. M. Gregor
    (Cambridge: Cambridge University Press, 1991), pp. 270, 482.

16 Kant, 'On the Common Saying: "This May Be True in Theory,
    but Does Not Apply in Practice"', p. 90. More specifically, this
    progress is a result of the antagonism inherent in every human
    being, in which we are driven towards both socialization and
    individualization (see especially Immanuel Kant, 'Idea for a
    Universal History with a Cosmopolitan Purpose', in *Political
    Writings*). This leads to conflicts in human societies, which in
    turn propel history and mankind forwards. The conflicts lead
    to revolutions and wars, but exactly these destructive events
    are positive from a historical perspective, and Kant argues
    that war is a tool for progress (Kant, *Critique of the Power
    of Judgement*, pp. 300, 433).

17 Kant, *Anthropology from a Pragmatic Point of View*, §61,
    pp. 103, 235.

18 Immanuel Kant, 'Reviews of Herder's Ideas on the Philosophy
    of the History of Mankind', in *Political Writings*.

19 Immanuel Kant, 'Perpetual Peace', in *Political Writings*,
    p. 116.

20 Kant, 'On the Common Saying: "This May Be True in Theory,
    but Does Not Apply in Practice"', pp. 89, 309f.

21 Theodor W. Adorno, *Negative Dialectics*, trans. E. B. Ashton
    (London: Routledge, 1973), p. 384ff.

22 Ibid., p. 276.

23 Ibid., p. 406.

24 Jonathan Lear, *Radical Hope* (Cambridge, MA: Harvard University Press, 2006), p. 97.

NINE Optimism, Pessimism and Hope

1 Václav Havel, *Disturbing the Peace*, trans. Paul Wilson (New York: Vintage, 1991), p. 181.

2 Václav Havel, *The Art of the Impossible*, trans. Paul Wilson (New York: Fromm International, 1997), p. 239.

3 Mara van der Lugt, *Dark Matters: Pessimism and the Problem of Suffering* (Princeton, NJ: Princeton University Press, 2021), especially ch. 2.

4 In that sense, it merges with the problem of theodicy in modern philosophy. I have discussed this in Lars Fr. H. Svendsen, *A Philosophy of Evil*, trans. Kerri Pierce (Champaign, IL/ London: Dalkey Archive Press, 2010), pp. 43–76.

5 Samuel Beckett, *Endgame: A Play in One Act* (New York: Grove Press, 1980), p. 44.

6 Arthur Schopenhauer, *The World as Will and Representation: Volume I*, trans. and ed. J. Norman and A. Welchman, ed. C. Janaway (Cambridge: Cambridge University Press, 2010), p. 423; Arthur Schopenhauer, *Parerga and Paralipomena: Volume II*, trans. and ed. A. Del Caro, ed. C. Janaway (Cambridge: Cambridge University Press, 2015), §156.

7 Schopenhauer, *The World as Will and Representation: Volume I*, p. 352.

8 Arthur Schopenhauer, *The World as Will and Representation: Volume II*, trans. J. Norman, A. Welchman and C. Janaway (Cambridge: Cambridge University Press, 2018), p. 598.

9 Schopenhauer, *Parerga and Paralipomena: Volume II*, §313.

10 Ibid., §153.

11 Schopenhauer, *The World as Will and Representation: Volume I*, p. 114.

12 Ibid., p. 338.

13 Schopenhauer, *The World as Will and Representation: Volume II*, p. 508.

14 Ludwig Wittgenstein, *Philosophical Investigations*, trans. G.E.M. Anscombe (Oxford: Blackwell, 1967), II.xi.

15 Jean-Jacques Rousseau, 'Letter from J.-J. Rousseau to Mr. de Voltaire, August 18, 1756', trans. Judith R. Bush et al., in

Mark Larrimore, ed., *The Problem of Evil: A Reader* (Oxford: Blackwell, 2001), p. 213.

16 François-Marie Arouet de Voltaire, *Candide*, trans. D. Gordon (Boston, MA: Bedford/St Martin's, 1999), p. 83.

17 *Havamal*, in Jackson Crawford, ed., *The Poetic Edda* (Indianapolis, IN: Hackett, 2015), verse 55, p. 27.

18 Ian Jarvie and Sandra Pralong, eds, *Popper's Open Society after Fifty Years* (London: Routledge, 1999), p. 40.

19 Erving Goffman, *The Presentation of Self in Everyday Life* (New York: Doubleday, 1959), p. 59.

20 Cf. Michael Ignatieff, *On Consolation: Finding Solace in Dark Times* (New York: Metropolitan Books, 2021), ch. 3.

21 Aristotle, *Nicomachean Ethics*, trans. W. D. Ross, in *The Complete Works of Aristotle*, vol. II (Princeton, NJ: Princeton University Press, 1985), 1106b19–24.

22 G.W.F. Hegel, *Enzyklopädie der philosophischen Wissenschaften* I, *Werke Band 8* (Frankfurt a.M.: Suhrkamp, 1986), §410. See also Aristotle, *Nicomachean Ethics*, 1152a25ff.

23 Nick Cave, 'The Red Hand Files #178', www.theredhandfiles. com, December 2021.

24 Nick Cave, 'The Red Hand Files #190', www.theredhandfiles. com, April 2022.

TEN Losing Hope

1 Theocritus, *Theocritus: Edited with a Translation and Commentary by A.S.F. Gow* (Cambridge: Cambridge University Press, 1952), verse 52, p. 37.

2 Cf. Anthony J. Steinbock, 'The Phenomenology of Despair', *International Journal of Philosophical Studies*, XV/3 (2007), p. 439.

3 Martin Heidegger, *Nietzsche*, trans. David Farrell Krell (San Francisco, CA: Harper and Row, 1991), p. 99.

4 Martin Heidegger, *Hölderlins Hymnen 'Germanien' und 'Der Rhein', Gesamtausgabe Band 39* (Frankfurt a.M.: Klostermann, 1980), p. 140.

5 Heidegger, *Hölderlins Hymnen 'Germanien' und 'Der Rhein'*, p. 89.

6 Martin Heidegger, *Being and Time*, trans. J. Stambough, revd edn (New York: SUNY Press, 2010), §29.

7 Heidegger, *Hölderlins Hymnen 'Germanien' und 'Der Rhein'*, p. 142.

8 Heidegger, *Being and Time*, §68в, p. 329.

9 See especially ibid., §31.

10 It is striking, however, that Heidegger, whose enormous
authorship comprises more than one hundred volumes,
barely mentions hope, beyond the short passage in *Being
and Time*, not least because it is a theme that should suit his
philosophy perfectly and where one can imagine two quite
different analyses of hope in the early and late periods of his
writing, where the early Heidegger would have advocated a
more active hope and the late Heidegger for a more passive
one. These analyses are nowhere to be found in his collected
works. Interestingly the expression 'hope' appears most often
as part of the expression 'hopeless' (*hoffnungslos*) when it
appears in his works, primarily as part of a description of
how one should not proceed when philosophizing. It is hard
to think of a factual reason why hope is mostly conspicu-
ous by its absence in Heidegger's works. It could be that the
term is too linked to Christian metaphysics for his taste. It is
worth noting that one place he uses the term 'hope' a handful
of times is his lectures on religious phenomenology, but in
a way that cannot shed significant light on what he writes
in *Being and Time* (Martin Heidegger, *Phänomenologie des
religiösen Lebens, Gesamtausgabe Band 60* (Frankfurt a.M.:
Klostermann, 1995)). To the extent that we can find some
kind of factual reason for the omission of hope in Heidegger's
analyses, it is enough that it can appear as a 'competitor' to
his preferred concepts of care in the early philosophy and
waiting in the late. The latter is supported by a fragment
in a recently published volume of sketches and drafts, in
which Heidegger actually mentions hope, claiming that
there is an abysmal difference between waiting and hoping,
and he rejects hope because it is an expression of what he
calls *Machenschaft*, a calculating way of being in which one
tries to control the world (Martin Heidegger, *Ergänzungen
und Denksplitter, Gesamtausgabe Band 91* (Frankfurt a.M.:
Klostermann, 2022), p. 662). However, it is so brief and
sketchily worded that it does not provide a basis for further
analysis.

11 Otto Friedrich Bollnow, *Das Wesen der Stimmungen*
(Frankfurt a.M.: Klostermann, 1995), p. 68.

12 Martin Heidegger, *Überlegungen XII–XV (Schwarze Hefte 1939–1941), Gesamtausgabe Band 96* (Frankfurt a.M.: Klostermann, 2014), p. 217.

13 Otto Friedrich Bollnow, *Neue Geborgenheit. Das Problem einer Überwindung des Existentialismus, Schriften Band 5* (Würzburg: Könighausen and Neumann, 2011), p. 57.

14 Bollnow wants to aim his critique at the very core of Heidegger's existential analysis by arguing that care will grasp at nothing without being given a direction by hope (ibid., p. 80). I'm not convinced that hope is more fundamental than care. More specifically, I cannot see that Bollnow has demonstrated that hope can function as a basic structure of temporality.

15 Ibid., p. 70.

16 Ibid., p. 76.

17 Primo Levi, *If This Is a Man*, trans. Stuart Woolf (London: Orion Press, 2007), pp. 203f.

18 Ibid., p. 144.

19 Ibid., p. 103.

20 Cf. Matthew Ratcliffe, *Experiences of Depression: A Study in Phenomenology* (Oxford: Oxford University Press, 2015), ch. 4. For an overview of current research, see Lorie A. Ritschel and Christopher S. Sheppard, 'Hope and Depression', in Matthew W. Gallagher and Shane J. Lopez, eds, *The Oxford Handbook of Hope* (Oxford: Oxford University Press, 2018).

21 Jens C. Thimm et al., 'Hope and Expectancies for Future Events in Depression', *Frontiers in Psychology*, IV (2013).

22 Cf. Shelley A. Fahlman et al., 'Does a Lack of Life Meaning Cause Boredom? Results from Psychometric, Longitudinal, and Experimental Analyses', *Journal of Social and Clinical Psychology*, XXVIII/3 (2009); Yael K. Goldberg et al., 'Boredom: An Emotional Experience Distinct from Apathy, Anhedonia, or Depression', *Journal of Social and Clinical Psychology*, XXX/6 (2011).

23 Fernando Pessoa, *The Book of Disquiet*, trans. Richard Zenith (New York: Penguin Books, 2003), p. 229.

24 Søren Kierkegaard, *Either/Or, Part 1*, trans. Howard V. Hong and Edna H. Hong (Princeton, NJ: Princeton University Press, 1987), p. 37.

25 Ibid., p. 290.

26 I have written more extensively about *acedia* in Lars Fr. H.
    Svendsen, *A Philosophy of Boredom*, trans J. Irons (London:
    Reaktion Books, 2005), pp. 49–52.
27 Jonathan Lear, *Radical Hope* (Cambridge, MA: Harvard
    University Press, 2006), p. 103.
28 Ibid., p. 39f.
29 Ibid., p. 97.
30 Ibid., p. 51.
31 Matthew Ratcliffe, 'What Is It to Lose Hope?', *Phenomenology
    and the Cognitive Sciences*, XII/4 (2013).
32 Cf. Matthew Ratcliffe, *Feelings of Being: Phenomenology,
    Psychiatry and the Sense of Reality* (Oxford: Oxford University
    Press, 2008).
33 Joseph Godfrey, *A Philosophy of Human Hope* (Dordrecht:
    Martinus Nijhoff, 1987), p. 3.
34 Gabriel Marcel, *The Philosophy of Existentialism*, trans. Manya
    Harari (New York: Citadel, 1995), p. 28.
35 Immanuel Kant, *Anthropology from a Pragmatic Point of View*,
    trans. M. Gregor (The Hague: Nijhoff, 1974), §76, p. 153.
36 Ludwig Wittgenstein, *Tractatus logico-philosophicus*, trans.
    D. F. Pears and B. F. McGuinness (London: Routledge, 1974),
    §6.43.
37 Ludwig Binswanger, 'Dream and Existence', trans. Jacob
    Needleman, *Review of Existential Psychology and Psychiatry*,
    XIX/1 (1984–5), p. 81.
38 E. M. Cioran, *A Short History of Decay*, trans. Richard Howard
    (London: Penguin Books, 2010), p. 25.
39 E. M. Cioran, *The Trouble with Being Born*, trans. Richard
    Howard (New York: Arcade Publishing, 1998), p. 54.
40 Cioran, *A Short History of Decay*, p. 88.

ELEVEN Hope and Meaning in Life

1 Albert Camus, *The Myth of Sisyphus and Other Essays*, trans.
   Justin O'Brien (London: Penguin Books, 1979).
2 Ibid., p. 94.
3 Ibid., p. 54.
4 Albert Camus, *Lyrical and Critical Essays*, trans. Ellen Conroy
   Kennedy (New York: Vintage Books, 1970), p. 92.
5 Peter Wessel Zapffe, *Om det tragiske* (Oslo: Pax, 2015), p. 18.
6 Ibid., p. 69.

7   Ibid., p. 99.

8   Ibid., p. 161; cf. p. 276.

9   Ibid., p. 181.

10 Peter Wessel Zapffe, 'Hvad er Tindesport?', in *Barske glæder* (Oslo: Pax, 1997), p. 96.

11 Galen Strawson, 'Against Narrativity', *Ratio*, XVII/4 (2004).

12 Ibid., p. 433.

13 Ibid., p. 431.

14 Galen Strawson, *Things That Bother Me: Death, Freedom, the Self, Etc.* (New York: New York Review of Books, 2018), p. 16f.

15 Quoted in Victor Bockris, *The Life and Death of Andy Warhol* (London: Fourth Estate, 1998), p. 225.

16 Galen Strawson, 'Episodic Ethics', in Daniel D. Hutto, ed., *Narrative and Understanding Persons* (Cambridge: Cambridge University Press, 2007), p. 109.

17 Paul Ricoeur, *Oneself as Another*, trans. K. Blamey (Chicago, IL/London: University of Chicago Press, 1994).

18 Christine Korsgaard, *The Sources of Normativity* (Cambridge: Cambridge University Press, 1996), p. 101.

19 Friedrich Nietzsche, *Twilight of the Idols*, in *The Anti-Christ, Ecce Homo, Twilight of the Idols and Other Writings*, trans. Judith Norman (Cambridge: Cambridge University Press, 2005), §12, pp. 19, 157.

20 Friedrich Nietzsche, *Thus Spoke Zarathustra*, trans. A. Del Caro (Cambridge: Cambridge University Press, 2006), p. 263.

21 Friedrich Nietzsche, *Beyond Good and Evil*, trans. Judith Norman (Cambridge: Cambridge University Press, 2002), §225, p. 116.

22 John Stuart Mill, *Utilitarianism*, in *Essays on Ethics, Religion and Society* (London: Routledge, 1969), p. 215.

23 Hans-Georg Gadamer, *Hermeneutische Entwürfe* (Tübingen: Mohr Siebeck, 2000), p. 218; cf. Hans-Georg Gadamer, *Wahrheit und Methode. Grundzüge einer philosophischen Hermeneutik. Gesammelte Werke Band 1* (Tübingen: J.C.B. Mohr, 1990), p. 355.

24 Percy Bysshe Shelley, *Prometheus Unbound*, in *The Major Works* (Oxford: Oxford University Press, 2009), part 4, verse 573f.

Bibliography

Adorno, Theodor W., *Negative Dialectics*, trans. E. B. Ashton (London: Routledge, 1973)

Allison, Henry E., *Kant's Theory of Freedom* (Cambridge: Cambridge University Press, 1990)

Aquinas, Thomas, *Summa theologiae*, Question 67, Article 4, Reply to Objection 2, https://aquinas101.thomisticinstitute.org

Arendt, Hannah, *The Human Condition* (Chicago, IL/London: University of Chicago Press, 1958)

——, *The Origins of Totalitarianism* (San Diego, CA/New York/London: Harcourt Brace and Company, 1979)

Aristotle, *Nicomachean Ethics*, trans. W. D. Ross, in *The Complete Works of Aristotle*, vol. II (Princeton, NJ: Princeton University Press, 1985)

——, *On Divination in Sleep*, trans. J. I. Beare, in *The Complete Works of Aristotle*, vol. I (Princeton, NJ: Princeton University Press, 1985)

——, *On Dreams*, trans. J. I. Beare, in *The Complete Works of Aristotle*, vol. I (Princeton, NJ: Princeton University Press, 1985)

——, *Rhetoric*, trans. W. Rhys Roberts, in *The Complete Works of Aristotle*, vol. II (Princeton, NJ: Princeton University Press, 1985)

——, *Sense and Sensibilia*, trans. J. I. Beare, in *The Complete Works of Aristotle*, vol. I (Princeton NJ: Princeton University Press, 1985)

Augustine, *The City of God*, trans. Marcus Dods (New York: Modern Library, 2000)

——, *Confessions*, trans. T. Williams (Indianapolis, IN: Hackett, 2019)

Beckett, Samuel, *Endgame: A Play in One Act* (New York: Grove
    Press, 1980)
Ben-Ze'ev, Aaron, *The Subtlety of Emotions* (Cambridge, MA: MIT
    Press, 2000)
Binswanger, Ludwig, 'Dream and Existence', trans. Jacob
    Needleman, *Review of Existential Psychology and Psychiatry*,
    XIX/1 (1984–5)
Bloch, Ernst, *The Principle of Hope*, trans. Neville Plaice, Stephen
    Plaice and Paul Knight, vol. I (Cambridge MA: MIT Press, 1995)
Bockris, Victor, *The Life and Death of Andy Warhol* (London:
    Fourth Estate, 1998)
Bollnow, Otto Friedrich, *Das Wesen der Stimmungen* (Frankfurt
    a.M.: Klostermann, 1995)
—, *Neue Geborgenheit. Das Problem einer Überwindung des
    Existentialismus, Schriften Band 5* (Würzburg: Könighausen
    and Neumann, 2011)
Bourke, Joanna, *Fear: A Cultural History* (London: Virago, 2005)
Bovens, Luc, 'The Value of Hope', *Philosophy and Phenomenological
    Research*, LVIII/3 (1999)
Bradley, Francis Herbert, *Aphorisms* (Oxford: Clarendon Press,
    1930)
Brod, Max, *Franz Kafka: A Biography* (New York: Schocken Books,
    1960)
Cairns, Douglas, 'Hope in Archaic and Classical Greek', in Claudia
    Blöser and Titus Stahl, eds, *The Moral Psychology of Hope*
    (London/New York: Rowman and Littlefield, 2020)
Camus, Albert, *Lyrical and Critical Essays*, trans. Ellen Conroy
    Kennedy (New York: Vintage Books, 1970)
—, *The Myth of Sisyphus and Other Essays*, trans. Justin O'Brien
    (London: Penguin Books, 1979)
Cassirer, Ernst, *An Essay on Man: An Introduction to a Philosophy
    of Human Culture* (New York: Doubleday, 1954)
Cave, Nick, 'The Red Hand Files #178', www.theredhandfiles.com
    (December 2021)
—, 'The Red Hand Files #190', www.theredhandfiles.com
    (April 2022)
Cioran, E. M., *Drawn and Quartered*, trans. Richard Howard
    (New York: Arcade Publishing, 1998)
—, *On the Heights of Despair*, trans. Ilinca Zarifopol-Johnston
    (Chicago, IL/London: University of Chicago Press, 1992)

—, *A Short History of Decay*, trans. Richard Howard (London: Penguin Books, 2010)

—, *The Trouble with Being Born*, trans. Richard Howard (New York: Arcade Publishing, 1998)

Crawford, Jackson, ed., *The Poetic Edda* (Indianapolis, IN: Hackett, 2015)

Descartes, René, *The Passions of the Soul*, in *The Philosophical Writings of Descartes*, trans. John Cottingham, Robert Stoothoff and Dugald Murdoch, vol. I (Cambridge: Cambridge University Press, 1985)

Dewey, John, 'Analysis of Reflective Thinking', in *The Later Works*, vol. VIII (Carbondale, IL: Southern Illinois University Press, 1986)

—, 'Liberalism and Social Action', in *The Later Works*, vol. XI (Carbondale, IL: Southern Illinois University Press, 1987)

Ehrenreich, Barbara, 'Pathologies of Hope', *Harper's Magazine*, 7 (February 2007)

Ekman, Paul, 'An Argument for Basic Emotions', *Cognition and Emotion*, VI/3–4 (1992)

Epictetus, *Handbook of Epictetus*, trans. Nicholas P. White (Indianapolis, IN/Cambridge: Hackett, 1983)

Fahlman, Shelley A., et al., 'Does a Lack of Life Meaning Cause Boredom? Results from Psychometric, Longitudinal, and Experimental Analyses', *Journal of Social and Clinical Psychology*, XXVIII/3 (2009)

Frankl, Viktor, *Man's Search for Meaning* (New York: Washington Square Press, 1985)

Fremstedal, Roe, 'Kierkegaard on Hope as Essential to Selfhood', in Claudia Blöser and Titus Stahl, eds, *The Moral Psychology of Hope* (London/New York: Rowman and Littlefield, 2020)

Gadamer, Hans-Georg, *Hermeneutische Entwürfe* (Tübingen: Mohr Siebeck, 2000)

—, *Wahrheit und Methode. Grundzüge einer philosophischen Hermeneutik. Gesammelte Werke Band 1* (Tübingen: J.C.B. Mohr, 1990)

Gallagher, Matthew W., and Shane J. Lopez, eds, *The Oxford Handbook of Hope* (Oxford: Oxford University Press, 2018)

Getty, J. Arch, and Oleg V. Naumov, *The Road to Terror: Stalin and the Self-Destruction of the Bolsheviks, 1932–39* (New Haven, CT/London: Yale University Press, 1999)

Godfrey, Joseph, *A Philosophy of Human Hope* (Dordrecht: Martinus Nijhoff, 1987)

Goethe, Johann Wolfgang von, 'An C. G. Voigt, Weimar 19. Dezember 1798', in Immanuel Kant, *Anthropologie in pragmatischer Hinsicht* (Hamburg: Felix Meiner, 1980)

——, *Faust, Part II*, trans. D. Constantine (London: Penguin Books, 2009)

Goffman, Erving, *The Presentation of Self in Everyday Life* (New York: Doubleday, 1959)

Goldberg, Yael K., et al., 'Boredom: An Emotional Experience Distinct from Apathy, Anhedonia, or Depression', *Journal of Social and Clinical Psychology*, XXX/6 (2011)

Havel, Václav, *The Art of the Impossible*, trans. Paul Wilson (New York: Fromm International, 1997)

——, *Disturbing the Peace*, trans. Paul Wilson (New York: Vintage, 1991)

Hegel, G.W.F., *Enzyklopädie der philosophischen Wissenschaften I*, *Werke Band 8* (Frankfurt a.M.: Suhrkamp, 1986)

Heidegger, Martin, *Being and Time*, trans. J. Stambough, revd edn (New York: SUNY Press, 2010)

——, *Die Grundbegriffe der Metaphysik, Welt, Endlichkeit, Einsamkeit, Gesamtausgabe Band 29/30* (Frankfurt a.M.: Klostermann, 1992)

——, *Ergänzungen und Denksplitter, Gesamtausgabe Band 91* (Frankfurt a.M.: Klostermann, 2022)

——, *Hölderlins Hymnen 'Germanien' und 'Der Rhein', Gesamtausgabe Band 39* (Frankfurt a.M.: Klostermann, 1980)

——, *Nietzsche*, trans. David Farrell Krell (San Francisco, CA: Harper and Row, 1991)

——, *Phänomenologie des religiösen Lebens, Gesamtausgabe Band 60* (Frankfurt a.M.: Klostermann, 1995)

——, *Überlegungen XII–XV (Schwarze Hefte 1939–1941), Gesamtausgabe Band 96* (Frankfurt a.M.: Klostermann, 2014)

Hesiod, *Works and Days*, in *Theogony/Works and Days/Testimonia*, trans. Glenn W. Most (Cambridge MA: Harvard University Press, 2006)

Hobbes, Thomas, *Leviathan* (Cambridge: Cambridge University Press, 1991)

——, *On the Citizen*, trans. Richard Tuck and Michael Silverthorne (Cambridge: Cambridge University Press, 1998)

Hosking, Geoffrey, *Trust: A History* (Oxford: Oxford University Press, 2014)

Hume, David, *Essays: Moral, Political, and Literary* (Indianapolis, IN: Liberty Fund, 1985)

—, *A Treatise of Human Nature* (London: Penguin Books, 1984)

Ignatieff, Michael, *On Consolation: Finding Solace in Dark Times* (New York: Metropolitan Books, 2021)

James, William, *The Will to Believe and Other Essays* (New York: Dover Publications, 1956)

Jarvie, Ian, and Sandra Pralong, eds, *Popper's Open Society after Fifty Years* (London: Routledge, 1999)

Kant, Immanuel, *Anthropology from a Pragmatic Point of View*, trans. M. Gregor (The Hague: Nijhoff, 1974)

—, *Anthropology, History, and Education*, trans. R. B. Louden and G. Zöller (Cambridge: Cambridge University Press, 2007)

—, *Correspondence*, trans. Arnulf Zweig (Cambridge: Cambridge University Press, 1999)

—, *Critique of the Power of Judgement*, trans. P. Guyer and E. Matthews (Cambridge: Cambridge University Press, 2002)

—, *Critique of Practical Reason*, trans. M. Gregor (Cambridge: Cambridge University Press, 2015)

—, *Critique of Pure Reason*, trans. P. Guyer and A. Wood (Cambridge: Cambridge University Press, 1998)

—, *The Metaphysics of Morals*, trans. M. Gregor (Cambridge: Cambridge University Press, 1991)

—, *Political Writings*, trans. H. B. Nisbet (Cambridge: Cambridge University Press, 1991)

—, 'Über das Mißlingen aller philosophischen Versuche in der Theodizee', in Preußischen Akademie der Wissenschaften, ed., *Kants gesammelte Schriften, Band 8* (Berlin/New York: de Gruyter, 1902ff)

Keynes, John Maynard, *A Tract on Monetary Reform* (Amherst, NY: Prometheus Books, 2000)

Kierkegaard, Søren, *Concluding Unscientific Postscript*, trans. Alastair Hannay (Cambridge: Cambridge University Press, 2009)

—, *Either/Or, Part 1*, trans. Howard V. Hong and Edna H. Hong (Princeton, NJ: Princeton University Press, 1987)

—, *Fear and Trembling*, trans. Alastair Hannay (New York: Penguin Books, 2006)

——, *Sickness unto Death*, trans. Howard V. Hong and
    Edna H. Hong (Princeton, NJ: Princeton University
    Press, 1980)

Korsgaard, Christine, *The Sources of Normativity* (Cambridge:
    Cambridge University Press, 1996)

Laertius, Diogenes, *Lives of Eminent Philosophers*, trans. Stephen
    White (Cambridge: Cambridge University Press, 2020)

Lear, Jonathan, *Radical Hope* (Cambridge, MA: Harvard University
    Press, 2006)

Levi, Primo, *If This Is a Man*, trans. Stuart Woolf (London: Orion
    Press, 2007)

Locke, John, *An Essay Concerning Human Understanding* (London:
    Penguin Books, 2004)

Lugt, Mara van der, *Dark Matters: Pessimism and the Problem of
    Suffering* (Princeton, NJ: Princeton University Press, 2021)

McGeer, Victoria, 'The Art of Good Hope', *Annals of the American
    Academy of Political and Social Science*, DXCII (2004)

Marcel, Gabriel, *The Philosophy of Existentialism*, trans. Manya
    Harari (New York: Citadel, 1995)

Martin, Adrienne, *How We Hope: A Moral Psychology* (Princeton,
    NJ: Princeton University Press, 2014)

Marx, Karl, *Critique of the Gotha Program*, in Lawrence H. Simon,
    ed., *Selected Writings* (Indianapolis, IN: Hackett, 1994)

Meirav, Ariel, 'The Nature of Hope', *Ratio*, XXII/2 (2009)

Mill, John Stuart, 'Theism', in *Essays on Ethics, Religion and Society*
    (London: Routledge, 1969)

——, *Utilitarianism*, in *Essays on Ethics, Religion and Society*
    (London: Routledge, 1969)

Miller, William Ian, *Outrageous Fortune: Gloomy Reflections on
    Luck and Life* (Oxford: Oxford University Press, 2021)

Milona, Michael, 'Finding Hope', *Canadian Journal of Philosophy*,
    XLIX/5 (2019)

Montaigne, Michel de, *The Essays of Michel Eyquem de Montaigne*,
    trans. Charles Cotton (Chicago, IL: Encyclopaedia Britannica,
    1952)

Nietzsche, Friedrich, *The Anti-Christ*, in *The Anti-Christ, Ecce
    Homo, Twilight of the Idols and Other Writings*, trans. Judith
    Norman (Cambridge: Cambridge University Press, 2005)

——, *Beyond Good and Evil*, trans. Judith Norman (Cambridge:
    Cambridge University Press, 2002)

—, *Dawn*, trans. Brittain Smith (Stanford, CA: Stanford University Press, 2011)

—, *Daybreak*, trans. R. J. Hollingdale (Cambridge: Cambridge University Press, 1986–97)

—, *Ecce Homo*, in *The Anti-Christ, Ecce Homo, Twilight of the Idols and Other Writings*, trans. Judith Norman (Cambridge: Cambridge University Press, 2005)

—, *The Gay Science*, trans. Josephine Nauckhoff (Cambridge: Cambridge University Press, 2001)

—, *Human, All Too Human,* trans. R. J. Hollingdale (Cambridge: Cambridge University Press, 1986)

—, *Thus Spoke Zarathustra*, trans. A. Del Caro (Cambridge: Cambridge University Press, 2006)

—, *Twilight of the Idols*, in *The Anti-Christ, Ecce Homo, Twilight of the Idols and Other Writings*, trans. Judith Norman (Cambridge: Cambridge University Press, 2005)

Ortony, Andrew, Gerald L. Clore and Allan Collins, *The Cognitive Structure of Emotions* (Cambridge: Cambridge University Press, 1998)

Pessoa, Fernando, *The Book of Disquiet*, trans. Richard Zenith (New York: Penguin Books, 2003)

Pettit, Philip, 'Hope and Its Place in Mind', *Annals of the American Academy of Political and Social Science*, DXCII (2004)

Plato, *The Laws of Plato*, trans. Thomas L. Pangle (Chicago, IL/ London: University of Chicago Press, 1988)

Popper, Karl R., *The Open Society and Its Enemies*, vol. I: *The Spell of Plato* (London: Routledge, 2005)

Ratcliffe, Matthew, *Experiences of Depression: A Study in Phenomenology* (Oxford: Oxford University Press, 2015)

—, *Feelings of Being: Phenomenology, Psychiatry and the Sense of Reality* (Oxford: Oxford University Press, 2008)

—, 'What Is It to Lose Hope?', *Phenomenology and the Cognitive Sciences*, XII/4 (2013)

Rawls, John, *Justice as Fairness: A Restatement* (Cambridge, MA: Harvard University Press, 2001)

—, *The Law of Peoples* (Cambridge, MA: Harvard University Press, 1999)

—, *Political Liberalism*, expanded edn (New York: Columbia University Press, 1996)

Ricoeur, Paul, *Oneself as Another*, trans. K. Blamey (Chicago, IL/
    London: University of Chicago Press, 1994)

Rioux, Catherine, 'Hope, Conceptual and Normative Issues',
    Philosophy Compass, XVI/3 (2021)

Ritschel, Lorie A., and Christopher S. Sheppard, 'Hope and
    Depression', in Matthew W. Gallagher and Shane J. Lopez, eds,
    The Oxford Handbook of Hope (Oxford: Oxford University
    Press, 2018)

Ritter, Bernhard, 'Solace or Counsel for Death', in Corey W. Dyck,
    ed., *Women and Philosophy in Eighteenth-Century Germany*
    (Oxford: Oxford University Press, 2021)

Rochefoucauld, François de La, *Collected Maxims and Other
    Reflections*, trans. E. H. Blackmore, A. M. Blackmore and
    Francine Giguére (Oxford: Oxford University Press, 2007)

Rousseau, Jean-Jacques, 'Letter from J.-J. Rousseau to Mr. de
    Voltaire, August 18, 1756', trans. Judith R. Bush et al., in
    Mark Larrimore, ed., *The Problem of Evil: A Reader* (Oxford:
    Blackwell, 2001)

Schlegel, Friedrich, *Lucinde*, trans. Peter Firchow (Minneapolis,
    MN: University of Minnesota Press, 1971)

Schlögel, Karl, *Moscow, 1937*, trans. Rodney Livingstone
    (Cambridge: Polity Press, 2012)

Schopenhauer, Arthur, *Parerga and Paralipomena: Volume II*,
    trans. and ed. A. Del Caro, ed. C. Janaway (Cambridge:
    Cambridge University Press, 2015)

—, *The World as Will and Representation: Volume I*, trans. and ed.
    J. Norman and A. Welchman, ed. C. Janaway (Cambridge,
    Cambridge University Press, 2010)

—, *The World as Will and Representation: Volume II*, trans. and ed.
    J. Norman, A. Welchman and C. Janaway (Cambridge:
    Cambridge University Press, 2018)

Segal, Gabriel, and Mark Textor, 'Hope as a Primitive Mental State',
    Ratio, XXVIII/2 (2015)

Shearer, David R., *Policing Stalin's Socialism, Repression and Social
    Order in the Soviet Union, 1924–1953* (New Haven, CT/London:
    Yale University Press, 2009)

Shelley, Percy Bysshe, *Prometheus Unbound*, in *The Major Works*
    (Oxford: Oxford University Press, 2009)

Shklar, Judith N., *Political Thought and Political Thinkers* (Chicago,
    IL/London: University of Chicago Press, 1998)

Snyder, C. R., 'The Past and Possible Futures of Hope', *Journal of Social and Clinical Psychology*, XIX/1 (2000)

Solomon, Robert C., 'Back to Basics: On the Very Idea of "Basic Emotions"', in *Not Passion's Slave: Emotions and Choice* (Oxford: Oxford University Press, 2003)

Sousa, Ronald de, 'Self-Deceptive Emotions', in Amélie Oksenberg Rorty, ed., *Explaining Emotions* (Berkeley, CA: University of California Press, 1980)

Spinoza, Baruch, *Ethics and Selected Letters*, trans. Samuel Shirley (Indianapolis, IN: Hackett, 1982)

——, *The Political Treatise*, in *The Collected Works of Spinoza*, trans. Edwin Curley, vol. II (Princeton, NJ: Princeton University Press, 2016)

——, *Short Treatise on God, Man, and His Well-Being*, in *Complete Works*, trans. Samuel Shirley (Indianapolis, IN: Hackett, 2002)

——, *Theological-Political Treatise*, trans. Michael Silverthorne and Jonathan Israel (Cambridge: Cambridge University Press, 2007)

Steinberg, Justin, *Spinoza's Political Psychology: The Taming of Fortune and Fear* (Cambridge: Cambridge University Press, 2018)

Steinbock, Anthony J., 'The Phenomenology of Despair', *International Journal of Philosophical Studies*, XV/3 (2007)

Stockdale, Katie, 'Emotional Hope', in Claudia Blöser and Titus Stahl, eds, *The Moral Psychology of Hope* (London/New York: Rowman and Littlefield, 2020)

Strawson, Galen, 'Against Narrativity', *Ratio*, XVII/4 (2004)

——, 'Episodic Ethics', in Daniel D. Hutto, ed., *Narrative and Understanding Persons* (Cambridge: Cambridge University Press, 2007)

——, *Things That Bother Me: Death, Freedom, the Self, Etc.* (New York: New York Review of Books, 2018)

Svendsen, Lars Fr. H., *A Philosophy of Boredom*, trans J. Irons (London: Reaktion Books, 2005)

——, *A Philosophy of Evil*, trans. Kerri Pierce (Champaign/London: Dalkey Archive Press, 2010)

——, *A Philosophy of Freedom*, trans. Kerri Pierce (London: Reaktion Books, 2014)

——, *Understanding Animals: Philosophy for Dog and Cat Lovers*, trans. Matt Bagguley (London: Reaktion Books, 2019)

Theocritus, *Theocritus: Edited with a Translation and Commentary by A.S.F. Gow* (Cambridge, Cambridge University Press, 1952)

Thimm, Jens C. et al., 'Hope and Expectancies for Future Events in Depression', *Frontiers in Psychology*, IV (2013)

Thucydides, *The Peloponnesian War*, trans. Martin Hammond (Oxford: Oxford University Press, 2009)

Voltaire, François-Marie Arouet de, *Candide*, trans. D. Gordon (Boston, MA: Bedford/St Martin's, 1999)

Walker, Margaret Urban, *Moral Repair: Reconstructing Moral Relations after Wrongdoing* (Cambridge: Cambridge University Press, 2006)

Walzer, Michael, 'On Negative Politics', in Bernard Yack, ed., *Liberalism without Illusions* (Chicago, IL/London: University of Chicago Press, 1996)

Weber, Max, *The Protestant Ethic and the 'Spirit' of Capitalism*, trans. Peter Baehr and Gordon C. Wells (London: Penguin Books, 2002)

Williams, Bernard, 'Truth, Politics, and Self-Deception', *Social Research*, LXIII/3 (1996)

Wittgenstein, Ludwig, *Philosophical Investigations,* trans. G.E.M. Anscombe (Oxford: Blackwell, 1967)

—, *Philosophical Occasions, 1912–1951*, ed. James C. Klagge and Alfred Nordmann (Indianapolis, IN: Hackett, 1993)

—, *Philosophische Bemerkungen. Werkausgabe in 8 Bänden*, Band 2 (Frankfurt a.M.: Suhrkamp, 1984)

—, *Philosophische Grammatik. Werkausgabe in 8 Bänden*, Band 4 (Frankfurt a.M.: Suhrkamp, 1984)

—, *Remarks on the Philosophy of Psychology*, vol. I (Oxford: Blackwell, 1983)

—, *Remarks on the Philosophy of Psychology*, vol. II (Oxford: Blackwell, 1983)

—, *Tractatus logico-philosophicus,* trans. D. F. Pears and B. F. McGuinness (London: Routledge, 1974)

Zapffe, Peter Wessel, 'Hvad er Tindesport?', in *Barske glæder* (Oslo: Pax, 1997)

—, *Om det tragiske* (Oslo: Pax, 2015)

Index of Names